2195

STREET

Schieffelin Hall

FOURTH STREET

Post Office

Summerfield Dry Goods

American Hotel

Otis Co. Hardware and Lumber

T.F. Ward Butcher

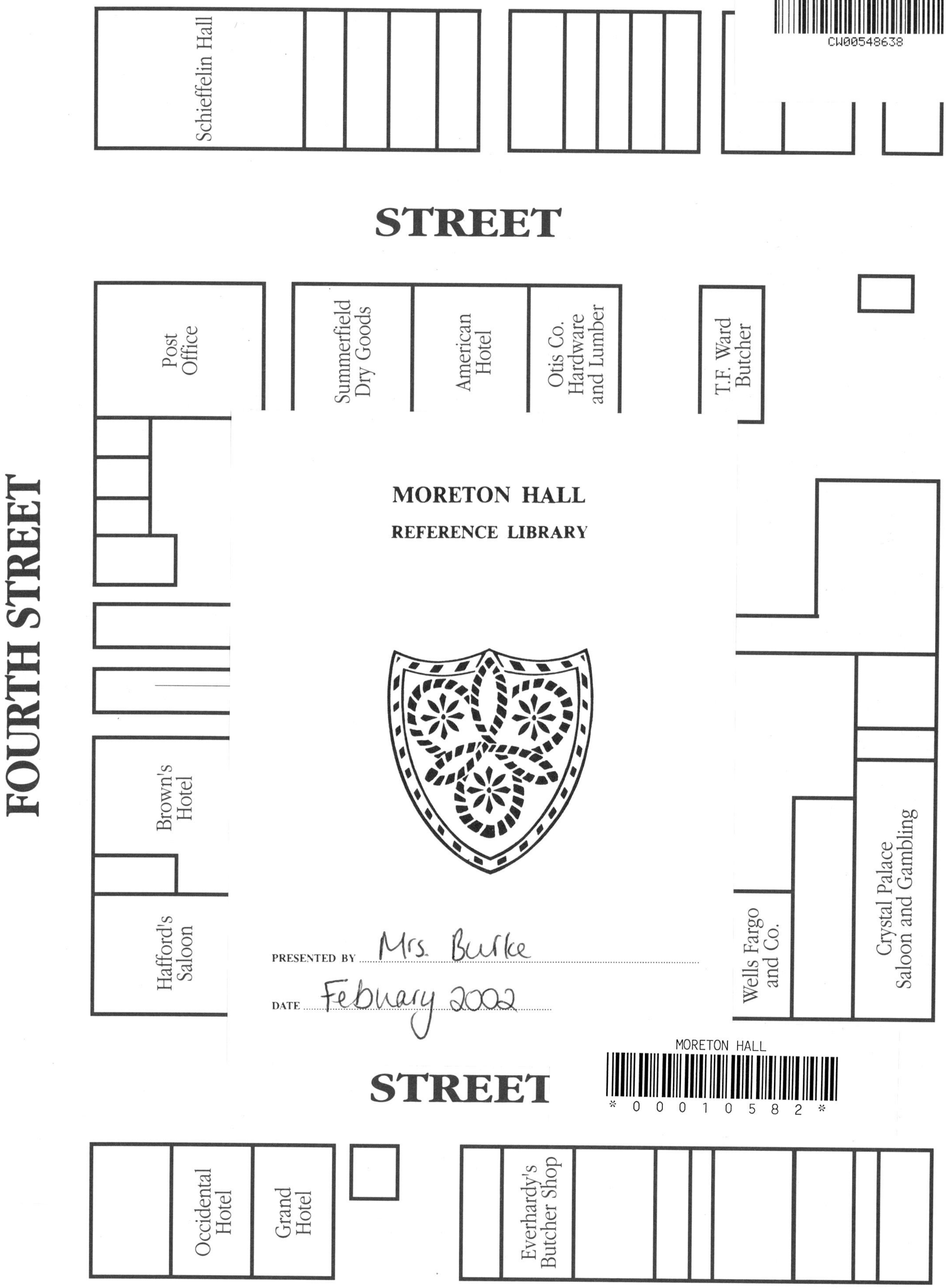

MORETON HALL

REFERENCE LIBRARY

Brown's Hotel

Hafford's Saloon

Wells Fargo and Co.

Crystal Palace Saloon and Gambling

PRESENTED BY _Mrs. Burke_

DATE _February 2002_

STREET

Occidental Hotel

Grand Hotel

Everhardy's Butcher Shop

"....about the old days, and the old ways...."

"....I am inclined toward profound sentiment. For I realize that in this age of fast-paced events, and of modern technology, there are but only a few places that remain where the old-timers may gather to talk about the old days, and the old ways, of that most redoubtable by-gone era of our nation's history. Tombstone is one of them."

Michael M. Hickey

Library of Congress Card Number 91-37748

ISBN 0-9631772-0-6

Copyright © 1991 by Michael M. Hickey

Manufactured in the United States of America

First Printing 1991

"Just another book about that Tombstone Shoot-out?

NO WAY!

All previous books and articles about the fatal fracas now known as the O.K. Corral Gunfight have contained, more or less accurately, general descriptions of that less-than-a-minute battle.

But now, in <u>Street Fight In Tombstone, Near the O.K. Corral</u>, author Michael M. Hickey ticks off, mini-second by mini-second, exactly what happened when the three brothers Earp and Doc Holliday....and the brothers Clanton and McLaury....faced off in that narrow rear entrance to the O.K. Corral.

Who fired first? Who was hit first? Who ran away? And what triggered it?

All the gripping detailed action is keyed to graphic and dramatic paintings by Master Artist and Illustrator Bruce R. Greene of Clifton, Texas.

Plus incisive vignettes of the principals in this tragic frontier drama....graphic descriptions by eyewitnesses....the sudden hush when the frantic firing stops.

Michael M. Hickey has pioneered a unique way to involve the reader in an historic event."

<u>THE TOMBSTONE EPITAPH</u>
The National Newspaper of the Old West
Founded May 1, 1880
Tombstone, Cochise County, Arizona

October 2, 1991

Michael M. Hickey

About the Author

International businessman, hotelier, entertainment entrepreneur, and author, Michael M. Hickey, 50, is a native of Honolulu, Hawaii. In 1949, he, his older brother, Patrick, along with their three sisters, Patricia, Maureen, and Bunny, accompanied their mother, Lucille, to her native Fiji Islands in the South Pacific for a planned three-month vacation that turned into a six-year stay for Michael. The Fiji experience was to have a profound and lasting effect on Mr. Hickey, which long-lived impressions were to directly influence his business activities in later years. While in Fiji, Mr. Hickey was schooled by British, Australian, and New Zealand tutors at the Boys' Grammar and Cadet School in Suva, Fiji's capital city, and was privileged to learn the language and the customs of his mother's homeland. Returning to Hawaii in the mid-1950's, Mr. Hickey finished his high schooling at the Marianist Brothers Catholic and R.O.T.C. all-boys institution, known in those days in Honolulu as St. Louis High School.

Promptly after graduation, Mr. Hickey enlisted in the U. S. Army Reserve and became a member of the World War II famed 'Go-For-Broke' 100th Battalion of the 442nd Infantry Regiment. Later he served on active duty with the 35th Infantry Regiment of the 25th Infantry 'Tropic Lightning' Division, headquartered at Schofield Barracks, on the island of Oahu, in Hawaii. Discharged from military service in December, 1964, Mr. Hickey entered the hotel industry in Waikiki as a desk clerk. But he quickly rose to the position of General Manager of the newly-opened, 550 room, Waikiki Outrigger Hotel, which property serves today as the flagship for the Outrigger Hotels Hawaii chain of almost 8,000 rooms, largest in the 50th State.

Forming his own consultancy in 1971, at age 30, Mr. Hickey was to manage and direct the operations of several world-class hotel and resort projects in the Pacific area; in Fiji; in Australia; and a six-month seconderment to a European hotel group based out of London, in the United Kingdom.

In 1980, as Chairman and Chief Executive of a group of trans-national corporations registered in Hawaii and in Hong Kong, Mr. Hickey and his business partners undertook a number of commercial ventures in the Pacific Ocean region with emphasis on economic development and capital improvement projects in Third World island nations. He continues with such activity today, albeit only on a select and limited basis.

Mr. Hickey's interest in the Old West, particularly the Tombstone era of the Earp Brothers and Doc Holliday and their legendary shoot-out with the Clantons and the McLaurys near the O.K. Corral, began in high school in the late 1950's. His enthusiasm for this most captivating chapter of Western Americana remained in a somewhat benign state, although he was to continue with his reading and research of the period, (as time allowed), during the three decades that spanned the 1960's, 70's, and the 1980's. However, in mid-March of this year, (1991), Mr. Hickey, in the company of long time friend and business associate, Allan K. Peralta, was to fulfill his boyhood dream of personally visiting Tombstone. It was this most inspiring rendezvous, with that mystical Frontier town, and with its warm and hospitable populace, that spurred Mr. Hickey to write Street Fight in Tombstone, Near the O.K. Corral, and to plan for its release in time for the 110th anniversary of the historic 30-second gunfight that happened a long time ago, on October 26, 1881.

Plates Two & Three

JOHN H. 'DOC' HOLLIDAY, 30, standing on Fremont Street, with long gray coat, cradles a sawed-off shotgun under his left arm, and, with his trademark nickel-plated Colt short-barreled revolver already in upward recoil in his right hand, has just unleashed a murderous shot into the stomach of Frank McLaury, at point blank range. Doc has started the historic 'Street Fight in Tombstone, Near the O.K. Corral'.

ROBERT F. 'FRANK' McLAURY, hit one inch to the left of the navel by Holliday, still clutches his revolver in a holster on his right hip, unable to draw as he absorbs the shock and horrific pain of the wound to his abdomen. Miraculously, Frank holds onto the reins of his horse, (on the street), with his left hand. He instinctively starts to grab for his gut with the same hand. Frank will scream. Spit blood. His shirt will smolder from the close-in effect of the powder burns. Frank's horse is panicked. Already off its feet, it will start

to pull the critically ailing Cowboy onto the street. In the process, the 33-year old McLaury will use the horse for cover, as he makes his way to the opposite side of the road, all the while escaping the soon-to-start pursuing fire of Doc Holliday and Morgan Earp.

MORGAN S. EARP, now positioned just outside the line of the boardwalks, to Doc Holliday's left, has his right shooting arm fully extended. His .45 Colt six-shooter is within a few feet of Billy Clanton. The 30-year old Morg has already fired the second shot of the infamous gun battle, so close to Doc's opening blast, that witnesses would have difficulty distinguishing between the two reports. Seeing Billy's quick reflexive action at pulling his (Clanton's) pistol at full cock to threaten Morgan's older brother, the Marshal, Virgil Earp, Morg will fire again, instantly, and with punishing effect at Billy.

WILLIAM HARRISON 'BILLY' CLANTON, will be thrown back on his right shoulder against the Harwood House as Morgan Earp's bullet will rip into his lung, just two inches left of the left nipple. But the young Cowboy will still show 'grit'. His six-gun already being pulled from its scabbard on his right hip, will discharge wildly in the direction of Virgil Earp, standing about ten feet to his front, holding a cane. Billy's right shooting hand is about to be shattered by a quick follow-up shot from Morgan Earp. Yet the game Cowboy is far from through. When rocked back against the Harwood building, with blood oozing from his left chest and broken gun hand, the 19-year old Clanton will still manage to switch his pistol to his left hand, and come out fighting.

WILLIAM 'BILLY THE KID' CLAIBOURNE, seen deepest in the vacant lot, is already racing for the walkway between the two Fly's structures. The so-called 'Arizona Billy The Kid' will skip into the back door of the larger rooming house to join Cowboy advocates, Sheriff John H. Behan, and William 'Billy' Allen, the latter believed responsible for creating the threat to back-shoot the Earps, to possibly cover the escape of Ike Clanton out of the area. The 21-year old Claibourne will sustain a gun shot 'nick' to his pants leg at the knee, (cloth only, no penetration of the flesh,) as he flees the shoot-out scene. This bullet is believed to have been accidentally fired out of Wyatt Earp's revolver in the opening seconds, as Ike Clanton lunged at Earp to hold his shooting arm away from the line of fire. In courtroom testimony later, Claibourne will state , "One bullet struck me on the knee of my pants".

THOMAS CLARK 'TOM' McLAURY, age 28, is barely seen in this illustration because the younger brother of Frank is already starting to maneuver behind Billy Clanton's horse, (inside vacant lot), jerking the bridle rein with him. The fear-stricken animal will prove difficult for Tom to handle, as it powers its way toward the main street. But McLaury will deftly move alongside of the horse, using it as a protective shield, to keep it between himself and the blistering Earp fusillade, until Tom, himself, can yank his own firearm, and shoot at Morgan Earp out toward the street.

VIRGIL W. EARP, the 38-year old Tombstone City Marshal, can be seen standing with his back to the street corner of Fly's Boarding House, holding the cane in his right hand. The presiding law officer of the Earp quartet opted to use the walking stick at first, to dramatize his demand for the Cowboys to surrender their guns, to avoid the very bloodshed now unfolding before him. But Virgil did not bargain for the homicidal plottings of Doc Holliday, and the equally hair-triggered Morgan Earp. For it was these latter two 'pistoleros' who were to start the tragic gunfight on the afternoon of October 26, 1881, 'law or no law', while the Marshal would look on seemingly frozen in disbelief. However, Virgil would be jolted out of his momentary transfixion as Morgan would soon come under attack from Tom McLaury, firing from behind the horse and over its saddle. The Marshal will then be targeted by Frank McLaury and Billy Clanton, two fatally wounded, but still ever-dangerous shooters, who will both regroup from their initial body wounds to join the withering street fire in earnest.

WYATT B. S. EARP, to Virgil's left, deeper in the vacant lot, with his left shoulder to the wall of the Fly's main building, has just been seized by Ike Clanton, these two antagonists about to engage in a brief joust of their own. As Ike grabbed for the 33-year old Wyatt's right arm to hold Earp's fully cocked long-barreled pistol away, the gun fired accidentally. This errant bullet probably gouged the pants leg of Billy Claibourne, seen in the background making a mad dash for the passageway behind Fly's Boarding House. As Cowboy leader Clanton would swear in court later, "....while I was holding him, (Wyatt Earp), he shot and I pushed him around the photograph gallery and jumped into the photograph gallery door...." (The author adheres to the opinion of a sizeable number of historians and researchers that Ike's reference to 'photograph gallery' actually means the front Boarding House of the two Fly's structures.) After pushing Wyatt against the wall of the Fly's building, Clanton will bolt right by the stupefied cane-wielding Virgil Earp, around the street corner of the house, into its front door.

JOSEPH ISAAC 'IKE' CLANTON, age 34, will flee the scene of the carnage and escape to safety. The braggart Cowboy chief will abandon his teenage brother, Billy, to die in a hail of bullets from the hated Earps. Running for his life at top speed, oblivious to everything else behind him, Ike will scramble through the streetside entrance of the larger Fly's hostelry; speed straight through the place, out of its rear door; enter the photo shack directly behind it; and, in a couple of giant strides, exit the back door of the little hut, eventually finding refuge in a building on Toughnut Street. The Earps and Doc Holliday would not make it easy for him. As the whiskey-sodden Clanton made his break through the door of the larger Fly's building, he would come under rapid fire strafing from Doc Holliday standing in the street, both of Doc's slugs barely missing. To hear Ike tell it in courtroom testimony after the gun battle, "....as I was leaving, and as I jumped into the door of the photograph gallery, (Boarding House), I heard one or two bullets pass right by my head...." Eyewitness, R. F. Coleman, put it this way, "....one shot fired at him, (Clanton), came pretty near to me, and struck a wagon standing in front of Bauer's shop. There was a second shot fired in that direction." Ike is shown without his hat on in this illustration to remind the reader that Clanton's head was believed bandaged at the time of the bloody affray, as the result of a rough-house pistol whipping near his right ear at the hands of the Marshal, Virgil Earp, about two hours earlier on Fourth Street.

To my sons, Mike, Jr., and Greg and Anthony Tukai in Fiji.

Just a little something to remember the old man.

And, to my Granddaughter, Talei.

Always remember your Great Grandmother, Lucille. She was a most remarkable woman of her time. The blood of her beloved Third World nation, Fiji, flows within you. She inspired your name, Talei, which translated means 'Most Precious'. Remember too, that the shadow you cast in life is that of your Noble ancestor. She walks with you. And because of it....you shall walk tall.

Michael M. Hickey

Street Fight
in
Tombstone

Near the O.K. Corral

STREET FIGHT IN TOMBSTONE,
Near the O.K. Corral

The Author:	Michael M. Hickey
Foreward contributed by:	Ben T. Traywick
Master Artist and Illustrator:	Bruce R. Greene
Project Supervisor and Production:	Terry Colbert, Ho'olauna Hawaii, Ltd.
Book Design:	James L. Peters
Computer Production:	Marvin P. Jastillana, James Peters Design Office
Printing Coordinator:	Richard W. Lyday, Sr.
The Publisher:	Talei Publishers, Inc.

For 110 years, researchers and historians of the Old West, book writers, and Hollywood moviemakers have all succumbed to the legend cast by that long shadow of what has become popularly known as 'The Gunfight at the O.K. Corral'. The controversy is as alive today as when it all began, even as the gunsmoke cleared and the dust settled amidst the wounded and dying on Fremont Street, in the silver mining camp of Tombstone, Arizona. It was Wednesday, October 26, 1881, after 2:00 p.m., on a cold, overcast afternoon.

When it started, four well-fashioned city dwellers, acting in the name of law and order, faced off against five defiant free-wheeling Cowboys, all of this in a vacant town lot affording no more than fifteen feet of space between the combatants. Add to such a tight-fitting death trap, almost two previous years of tension-filled harassments, fight talk, and near-gunfire close calls between the two rival factions, and you have the makings of the most famous shoot-out in the history of the Old West.

When it was over, three Cowboys lay dying in the street. Two others escaped to safety. Three of the Lawmen's party were wounded. And one, Wyatt Earp, stood unscathed.

But, in only those 'thirty seconds with about thirty shots fired', who shot who? When? Where did they fall? Why? These questions have persisted for over a century....and the debate continues.

Now, someone has stepped forward to tackle this hotly contested issue. Head on. <u>STREET FIGHT IN TOMBSTONE, Near the O.K. Corral</u>, is a no-holds-barred, spine-

Street Fight in Tombstone,

Near the O.K. Corral

chilling, bullet-by-bullet account of what its author believes actually happened, and between whom, in that murderous half minute, a long time ago. Read it. Feel it. Experience the ear-shattering staccato of six-shooters, and of a double-barreled shotgun, all blasting away at point blank range, such awesome weapons wielded by lightning fast, skilled shootists of that violent era. You can almost hear the bullets impacting, and the blood-curdling sounds of the wounded and dying, all around you.

And when you finally put this book down, you too will sense that author Michael M. Hickey had just taken you back in time to over a century ago and placed you right in the heart of the most talked about 'thirty seconds' in the turbulent history of the American Frontier.

Foreword

By Ben T. Traywick

This volume by Michael M. Hickey is certainly not like the dozens of others that have been written about the confrontation called "Gunfight at O.K. Corral". That does not mean that it or the others are wrong - only different.

Hickey is a newcomer to the field of Earpiana. But this first publication gives a fresh look at the details of the most famous gunfight of the American West. He offers a plausible explanation as to how these legendary events could have occurred.

Let us take a better look at these men who were known as the 'Earp party' on the one side, and those known as the 'Cowboys' on the opposing side.

Many people who have studied much about Western Americana have read volumes concerning 'The Fighting Earps', but few are aware that there were five Earp brothers and a half brother.

NEWTON JASPER EARP, the half brother and the eldest, was born in Hartford, Kentucky, October 7, 1837. Most who have valid claims of being related to the Earp family are descendants of Newton, as he had several children. Virgil had one daughter. The other brothers had none that reached adulthood. Newton died in Sacramento, December 18, 1928, and is buried there.

JAMES COOKSEY EARP, oldest of the full brothers, was born in Hartford, Kentucky, June 28, 1841. During the war between the States, he served in Company F, Seventeenth Illinois Infantry. James was wounded in Missouri in 1861, and as a result, had a crippled left arm the remainder of his life. James moved about the country with 'The Fighting Earps', but was physically unable to be involved in their affairs, and was usually a bartender or a gambler. He died in Los Angeles, January 25, 1926, and is buried in San Bernardino.

VIRGIL WALTER EARP was born in Hartford, Kentucky, July 18, 1843. During the war between the States, he served in Company C, Eighty-Third Illinois Infantry, and was discharged in Nashville in June, 1865. While a U.S. Deputy Marshal and the Town Marshal of Tombstone, he was wounded in the Gunfight at O.K. Corral. Later that year, (1881), he was crippled for life by an ambush near the Crystal Palace Saloon. Virgil received a pension of $12 a month, believed to be partial recompense for the wound he received in Tombstone, and also as a veteran of the Civil War. He died in Goldfield, Nevada, October 20, 1905, and is buried in Portland, Oregon.

WYATT BERRY STAPP EARP was born in Monmouth, Illinois, March 19, 1848. It was actually Wyatt Earp who was the leader of 'The Fighting Earps'. He was sometimes a lawman, but mostly a gambler. At times, he dealt in real estate and owned race horses. He followed the gold rush to Alaska. He spent the last years of his life prospecting near the Colorado River. All his life, Wyatt was a controversial character. There were those who liked and respected him. And there were those who hated him. There was no middle ground. Wyatt died in Los Angeles, January 13, 1929. He is buried in Colma, California.

MORGAN S. EARP was born in Pella, Iowa, April 24, 1851. This younger brother followed in the footsteps of Wyatt as lawman, gambler, and Wells Fargo shotgun guard. Morgan was hot tempered, prone to violence, and friendly with Doc Holliday. The two of them spent considerable time gambling in the towns around Tombstone. He was seriously wounded in the Gunfight at O.K. Corral. On March 18, 1882, he was killed by an assassin, shooting from the darkness of an alley, while playing billiards with Bob Hatch in Campbell and Hatch's Saloon in Tombstone. His body was shipped by train to Colton, California, for burial.

BAXTER WARREN EARP, the youngest of the brothers, was born in Pella, Iowa, March 9, 1855. He did not become involved in his brother's problems until after the gunfight. He did ride with Wyatt on his bloody trail of vengeance in the spring of 1882. Warren was killed by a cowhand named John Boyett, in a Willcox saloon on July 6, 1900. There is substantial evidence that this shooting may have been murder, as Warren was unarmed. He is buried in Willcox, Arizona.

And now, a look at the men who faced the Earps and Doc Holliday in the gunfight, the men that most of us know as the 'Cowboys'.

JOSEPH ISAAC CLANTON, spokesman for the Cowboy faction, was born in Calloway County, Missouri, in 1847. The Clanton family was to have eight children. Ike and Billy, (WILLIAM HARRISON CLANTON), the youngest, were the only two of the Clantons involved in the street fight with the Earps. Billy was born in Texas in 1862. He did not survive the gunfight on October 26, 1881, in Tombstone.

In 1877, the Clanton family moved to a ranch on the San Pedro River, a few miles from where Tombstone was soon to appear. They prospered by doing some ranching and a little freighting. Ike survived the O.K. Corral gunfight, only to die on June 1, 1887, while trying to evade arrest for rustling. He is buried on the Blue River, where he was felled by lawman C. V. Brighton's bullet.

Before long, two young brothers, Tom and Frank McLaury, moved to the San Pedro as neighbors to the Clantons. They became friendly with the Clantons and sometimes did business with them.

The McLaury brothers had been born into a family that had eleven children. ROBERT FINDLEY (FRANK) McLAURY, was born March 3, 1848, and THOMAS CLARK McLAURY, June 30, 1853, both in Korthright, New York. The boys were from a good family. Certainly they were not of the same trouble-prone breed as the Clantons. It is difficult to understand how they became involved with them.

Progressively the two brothers became party to the questionable activities of the Clantons. N. J. 'OLD MAN' CLANTON gave his ranch, (on the San Pedro River), to his boys, late in 1880, and moved into the Animas Valley in New Mexico, very near the Mexican border. The McLaury brothers sold their ranch to John Slaughter, and took up property near Soldiers Hole in the Sulphur Springs Valley, about the same time. With these calculated moves, the Clantons and McLaurys could enhance and control their rustler activities in and out of Arizona, New Mexico, and below the border in and out of Mexico itself.

Two who were involved in the O.K. Corral gunfight, but belonged to neither family, were John H. Holliday and William Claibourne.

JOHN H. 'DOC' HOLLIDAY, staunch friend of the Earps, was born in Griffin, Georgia, August 14, 1851. He was educated as a dentist, graduating from the Pennsylvania College of Dental Surgery in Philadelphia, class of 1872. Not long after, he discovered that he had tuberculosis and moved west, where he gradually gave up dentistry in favor of gambling. He died of tuberculosis in Glenwood Springs, Colorado, November 8, 1887, and is buried there.

WILLIAM CLAIBOURNE came up the trail from Texas with one of John Slaughter's cattle herds. Soon after his arrival he made friends with the Cowboys. He was present in Tombstone at the time of the confrontation with the Earps. But when the shooting started, he quickly decided that he 'wasn't all that concerned', and hastily departed the scene. Unfortunately, he did not show the same intelligence on November 14, 1882. When he threatened 'Buckskin Frank' Leslie, he, (Claibourne), was sent to his final reward, post haste, with a well-aimed bullet to the side of his body.

It is evident that the men involved in this bloody spectacle were tough, brash, self-reliant, independent, and determined individuals. Some insist that the Earps were not lily white, and that the Cowboys were victims of their time. Perhaps......

Ben T. Traywick

Author of The Chronicles of Tombstone.

Resident-Historian, City of Tombstone, Arizona.

Researcher in Earpiana.

June 22, 1991

Thank you ,
Rose Marie Lepere Frank,
without whom this work would
not be possible.

It is said that the fine line between Love and Hate is so minute as to be indiscernible. Both emotions often conflict to the extreme. Yet the connection, the umbilical cord, between the two is indelible. The two are one. And it is Love, by the nature of things in life, that is destined to always emerge. Hate is its aberration. Its flaw. So it is with the two of us, Rose. Thank you, my proud, indomitable, long-time Sicilian secretary; administrative assistant; personal friend; confidante; antagonist; guardian of my security interests; and above all, devoted servant to my pre-eminent late mother, Lucille. Thank you and God Bless You for all of it. At the time of the final sunset, remember that, The Man, Michael M. Hickey, who you chose to devote a significant part of your life and career to protect, was, after all....

just a man.

THEY SHOT THEIR WAY INTO HISTORY

The Earp Brothers and Doc Holliday

Hear Ye! Hear Ye! Judge them not my friend,
When they are called, they shoot to kill.
If they survive the street fight, be it a Godsend,
If they should die, bury them in Boot Hill.

In the annals of the Frontier, they stood alone.
The Earp Brothers and Doc Holliday.
One can sense their presence in Tombstone.
For they still walk the streets this day.

Down Fourth, to turn west on Fremont Street,
They faced the Cowboys in the vacant lot.
At point blank range, with no retreat,
Doc Holliday fired the opening shot .

"Give me some more cartridges", pleaded Billy, too late,
The McLaury's, Frank and Tom, lay dying where they fell.
For the three brave Cowboys, such was their fate,
They fought to the end. And they died well.

Thirty seconds with about thirty shots fired, t'was a real test,
Virg, Morg, and Doc wounded. Wyatt not touched at all.
In the most famous gunfight of the American West,
The Earp Brothers and Doc Holliday answered the call.

Whatever their stuff, they were men of their time,
They are called cowards, or knights of chivalry.
But their legendary bell will forever chime,
They shot their way into history.

TABLE OF ILLUSTRATIONS

TABLE OF CONTENTS

Part One

Part Two

Editorial

LANGUAGE OF THE GUNFIGHTER

"IF YOU EVER COME AFTER ME YOU WILL NEVER TAKE ME."
Frank McLaury to Morgan Earp several days before the street fight.

"YOU SON-OF-A-BITCH OF A COWBOY, GET YOUR GUN OUT AND GET TO WORK."
Doc Holliday to Ike Clanton the evening before the street fight.

"YOU MAY HAVE TO FIGHT BEFORE YOU KNOW IT."
Ike Clanton to Virgil Earp the evening before the street fight.

"AS SOON AS THOSE DAMNED EARPS AND DOC HOLLIDAY SHOW THEMSELVES ON THE STREET, THE BALL WILL OPEN."
Ike Clanton about two hours before the street fight.

"FIGHT IS MY RACKET. ALL I WANT IS FOUR FEET OF GROUND."
Ike Clanton to Wyatt Earp just over an hour before the street fight.

"IF YOU WANT TO FIGHT, I AM WITH YOU."
Tom McLaury to Wyatt Earp one hour before the street fight.

"LOOKS LIKE REAL TROUBLE."
John P. Clum, Mayor of the City of Tombstone.

"THERE ARE A LOT OF SONS-OF-BITCHES IN TOWN LOOKING FOR A FIGHT."
Virgil Earp to Sheriff John H. Behan less than an hour before the street fight.

"LET THEM HAVE IT."
Morgan Earp to Doc Holliday less than one minute before the street fight.

"YOU SONS-OF-BITCHES HAVE BEEN LOOKING FOR A FIGHT, NOW YOU CAN HAVE IT."
Morgan Earp to the Cowboys just seconds before the start of the shooting.

"THIS IS NONE OF OUR FIGHT. WE HAD BETTER GET OUT OF HERE."
Robert Hatch, Saloon Keeper, just seconds after the shooting started.

"I'M HIT."
Morgan Earp having just been shot through the shoulders.

"I'VE GOT YOU NOW."
Frank McLaury to Doc Holliday during the shooting.

"YOU'RE A GOOD ONE IF YOU HAVE."
Doc Holliday back to Frank McLaury during the shooting.

"I'M SHOT RIGHT THROUGH."
Doc Holliday having just been shot by Frank McLaury.

"YOU HAVE GOT IT NOW."
Eyewitness R.F. Coleman calling out to Doc Holliday as he, (Coleman),
watched the lethal exchange between Doc Holliday and Frank McLaury.

"I GOT HIM."
Morgan Earp claiming to have just shot Frank McLaury in the head.

"GIVE ME SOME MORE CARTRIDGES."
Billy Clanton in the throes of death to C. S. Fly as the shooting ended.

*"...AND I NATURALLY KEPT MY EYES OPEN FOR I DID NOT INTEND THAT ANY OF
THE GANG SHOULD GET THE DROP ON ME IF I COULD HELP IT."*
Wyatt Earp, several weeks after the street fight.

Plate Four

WYATT EARP. How many people in the civilized world have been named Wyatt Earp? He couldn't have been given a more recognizable moniker, like, say, a John Smith....a Robert Thompson....or a Henry Jones. No offense intended to those gentlemen so labeled, but a name as unique, as defiant, as WYATT EARP, just does not seem to belong with the rest of us mortals.

WYATT EARP. One can never say it enough. It is that one-of-a-kind type of brand that vaults right out at you from the turbulent pages of our Frontier past. As soon as you pronounce it, you know, deep in your boyish heart of Western Americana, that Wyatt Earp is destined to survive the ages. It is the very stuff of legends. A made-to-order Hollywood script. A book writer's dream. A never-ending challenge to get at the truth. But the truth seems to evade. We will never be satisfied. The search continues for WYATT EARP, Superstar.

Add to the phantom aura of such a name the tall, handsome, dark-suited, mustached Man of the Gun, depicted in the actual photo-inspired illustration that accompanies this chapter, and the possibilities are endless. Talk about show biz.

Just look at him. If dark glasses were in fashion in those days, WYATT EARP would surely be first to sport them, as naturally, and as indelibly as he carried his death-wielding six-guns. Wyatt Earp and dark glasses would go together. If there existed a C.I.A. or an F.B.I., or some such top secret security organization, during those wild and wooly times, then you can bet the ranch that the hearsay alone would place WYATT EARP at the center of such clandestine company. And, as if not to be denied, if there was then a Cosa Nostra, a brotherhood of evil doings, a sort of crime syndicate of the Old West, then, the gossip all around the desert cactus would have WYATT EARP as its 'Boss of all Bosses'.

"Again and again, her, (Mrs. Virgil Earp's), gaze would come to rest on Wyatt. With his narrow face and long drooping mustaches, his slender gambler's hands and secretive air, he seemed to focus all the mystery of their, (Earp brother's), guarded talk....later on I found out some things about him I won't ever tell to my dying day, so I know I was right. All those books makin' him out a big hero are pure gingerbread." (These words are attributed to Virgil Earp's wife, Allie, in the Frank Waters' book, The Earp Brothers of Tombstone.)

For those who believe in the reincarnative experience, and in communications within the psychic realm, now is the time to put all of your mystifying forces to work, to do all in your powers to bring WYATT EARP back to us in this lifetime. To say the least, we have a few million questions to ask him.

Not content to assuage us idol-worshipers with the usual John Wayne wide sombrero, colorful kerchief swagger, so well known to Western movie buffs who had come to identify such attire with that tumultuous period of our history, WYATT EARP, well, he sort of looks different. Dark hat. Dark Prince Albert coat. Dark vest. Dark trousers outside of fine dark leather half boots. Dark shoe-string tie on a brilliant white dress shirt. And his complexion? Not dark. Blond. All six feet of him. What thoughts must have lurked behind the curious stares of the inhabitants of Tombstone 110 years ago, to see such a ghost-like countenance stroll their streets, and to know that this was the law in that hellish desert metropolis. Behold ye woman, you of the flirtatious glance and the cheeky smile, curb thy fantasy. And you, reckless youth and ambitious gunslinger, don't even try it.....unless you covet an ambition to die young. WYATT EARP, lady killer. WYATT EARP, man killer.

"The Lion of Tombstone" is what writer, Walter Noble Burns, called WYATT EARP. Maybe so. His hair, mustache, and his eyebrows, may have regaled the tawny blond of the King of the Beasts, but there was the quickness, the stealth, of the black panther, too...and all of the mystery that stalks with it.

His detractors, and there are many, call him an exhibitionist. "Wyatt was an itinerant saloon keeper, card sharp, gunman, bigamist, church deacon, policeman, bunko artist, and supreme confidence man", writes Earp cynicist Frank Waters, in The Earp Brothers of Tombstone. Looking at WYATT EARP all decked out in his fashionable wardrobe, one might be inclined to instantly agree. But, where is the gun that a viewer might be prone to associate with such an audacious display? You will not find any insidious killing devices flaunted here. But, it is there. Make no mistake about it. They say that our salient one-of-a-kind upholder of law and order was inclined to favor a .45 Colt single action pistol, with a seven-and-one-half inch barrel, blue steel, well worn, with a wooden handle, which the slang of the Frontier dubbed the 'Hog-leg'. Tucked discreetly away in a special slit-pocket at the waist inside of his long-coat, this was an awesome weapon, that its skilled lightning-fast practitioner, WYATT EARP, would bend over some unruly and testy Cowboy's thick skull, repeatedly, throughout his storied career. For, to club a law breaker senseless, is to take the sting out of his acid tongue. De-fang and humiliate the ruffian, rather than to shoot to kill him. Such was the way of our story-book Marshal, as the record shows, again, and again. Just when you feel you had finally pegged WYATT EARP for a back-shooter and a murdering horse thief, the just-mentioned record of propensity for non-violence over brutal killing 'smacks you in the chops', and reminds you that all is not what his enemies would have us believe. For such Earp-haters have tagged Wyatt for practically every crime from highway robbery to murder during his danger-filled Tombstone stint as a part-time Peace Officer.

Those who are destined to stand alone, and apart, always seem to get the blame.

"All the Earps were professional gamblers. They were charged, first and last, with almost half of the robberies that were of such frequent occurrence on the roads leading out of the camp", asserted James H. McClintock, Arizona State Historian, in story teller Alford E. Turner's, The Earps Talk.

"Wyatt Earp continues to be a misunderstood man, and probably will remain so to many people. He was more of a businessman than a lawman and a gunfighter, yet most reporting about him concerns violence", rebuts the same Earp expert, Alford E. Turner, in his book, The Earps Talk.

"You ask my impressions about Wyatt Earp in Tombstone as a Peace Officer and as a man. As a man he was Ace high, and as a Peace Officer he WAS the peace", so swears Fred J. Dodge, the career undercover agent for Wells Fargo in the book, Undercover for Wells Fargo by Carolyn Lake.

WYATT EARP. Love him or hate him. How is it possible that one man, a human being if you will, could enthrall so many for so long? And we ain't seen nothing yet. For as sure as the sun rises, and the morning tide surges, the debate will continue. How blessed are those lesser knowns in their weed-infested Boot Hill graves, strewn across our ghost-like frontier. They rest in peace. Consigned to the inviolable serenity of their pasts, they are forgotten. But not so with WYATT EARP. It shall never come to pass that this most mythical of Old West characters be obliterated from memory.

In Glenn G. Boyer's outstanding narrative, I Married Wyatt Earp, here is what Mrs. Wyatt 'Josie' Earp had to say about an incident just two weeks before the death of her 80-year old husband in Los Angeles. "He, (Wyatt), had been lying quietly for some time, his eyes and mind far away. Suddenly he raised up on his elbow, looking through me rather than at me, and said, 'Supposing....supposing'. What is it Wyatt?, I asked, concerned about his appearance. The light went out of his eyes, and he fell back on the pillow. 'Oh, well!', he said in a resigned fashion."

And the secrets were to go with him.

"The real story of the Old West can never be told unless Wyatt Earp will tell what he knows; and Wyatt will not talk", so said William Barclay 'Bat' Masterson, himself a much chronicled Frontier Peace Officer and Earp loyalist.

Many years ago, one of my bosses said this to me, "Michael, beware of the man who is liked by everybody. Such a man is usually not capable of making the decisions that really count. Because the tough calls in life do not....cannot....please all people".

WYATT EARP is not liked by everybody.

Yet, the minds and hearts of men shall not be free of him. It is never so with heroes. Whether he had any foretelling or ambition to be thusly singled out, he has become the very institution itself, the symbol of the ways of his time. For Wyatt Earp IS the Old West. It lives on as he lives on.

And in the mind and heart of this author, WYATT EARP WALKS TALL.

Michael M. Hickey
Honolulu, Hawaii
May 24, 1991

"MY GOD, MRS. EARP, GET AWAY!
THERE'S BEEN AN AWFUL FIGHT!"

"Lou (Mrs. Morgan 'Louisa' Earp) and me was sewin'....
when all of a sudden guns started roarin'. The noise
was awful it was so close - just a couple of short blocks
up Fremont. Lou laid down her hands in her lap and
bent her head. I jumped up and ran out the door. I
knew it had come at last....

I flew up the street. People all over were runnin'
toward the O.K. Corral....One of the McLaury brothers
was lyin' dead on the corner of Third Street....I never
stopped runnin' past him....Bunches of people were col-
lectin' in front of the corral. One of them was carryin'
Billy Clanton across the street. He was a young boy,
only nineteen, and he was dyin'.

I ran to the next bunch. Just then a man grabbed me.
A lawyer named Harry Jones. 'My God, Mrs. Earp, get
away! There's been an awful fight'."

Mrs. Virgil 'Allie' Earp.
From her residence at the
corner of Fremont and First Streets,
as quoted in the Frank Waters book,
The Earp Brothers of Tombstone.

THE EVENT:
Historically known as, 'The Gunfight at O.K. Corral'.

THE PLACE:
Tombstone, Arizona

THE DAY AND DATE:
Wednesday, October 26, 1881

THE TIME OF DAY:
After 2:00 p.m. on a dull, overcast day. Cold. Winter chill already in the air.

THE LOCATION:
In a vacant lot on Fremont Street, between Fly's Boarding House to the east, with the Harwood House to the west. The fight spilled onto Fremont Street as far west as the corner of Third and Fremont, and, as far east as the front of Fly's Boarding House.

THE COMBATANTS:
The Earp Brothers and Doc Holliday.

VIRGIL 'VIRG' WALTER EARP (38)
City Marshal of Tombstone.

WYATT B. S. EARP (33)
Acting Marshal (in Virgil's absence from Tombstone).

MORGAN 'MORG' S. EARP (30)
Special Policeman

JOHN HENRY 'DOC' HOLLIDAY (30)
Deputized for the purpose of assisting Marshal Virgil Earp in this street fight

The Cowboys

JOSEPH ISAAC 'IKE' CLANTON (34)
Rancher - Cattle Rustler (Cowboy)

WILLIAM HARRISON 'BILLY' CLANTON (19)
Brother of Ike (Cowboy)

ROBERT FINDLAY 'FRANK' McLAURY (33)
Rancher - Cattle Rustler (Cowboy)

THOMAS CLARK 'TOM' McLAURY (28)
Brother of Frank (Cowboy)

WILLIAM 'BILLY THE KID' CLAIBOURNE (21)
Millworker and Wagon Driver - Friend of the Cowboys

Part One

The Combatants

THE INEVITABLE CONFLICT

The City Marshal's group had been at legal, political, and now personal, odds with the Cowboy elements who depredated around the Cochise County countryside surrounding Tombstone. The Earp brothers began to settle in the city on December 1, 1879. By the end of the summer of the following year, Virgil, Wyatt, and Morgan Earp, along with their spouses and families, including older brother James, were firmly entrenched in the community. Wyatt's friend and gambling sidekick, Doc Holliday, accompanied by his mistress, 'Big Nosed' Kate Elder, had also relocated to Tombstone.

The Earps were politically and financially connected with a sector of the Tombstone elite, including the gambling fraternity of that city. The brothers were all Republicans. Their manner, style, and habiliments were typical of fashionable city dwellers. In a short period of time, Virgil was appointed City Marshal (1880). Morgan was a shotgun guard on the Wells Fargo stages. Wyatt already held a Deputy Sheriff's appointment. But he coveted the newly-created Cochise County Sheriff's position, also being contested by John H. Behan, a Democrat, and a confidante of the Cowboy crowd, themselves all Democrats.

It was generally suspected that 'The Clantons' and 'The McLaurys', (in league with such notorious gun-slingers as John P. Ringo, and William 'Curly Bill' Brocius), were operating a cattle rustling ring by 'recycling' stolen Mexican cattle from across the border, re-branding the stock, and then selling the just-acquired herds to Army posts, or to nearby ranches, or to any takers, at bargain prices.

The rough-house, and, at times, unsophisticated Clanton-McLaury Cowboys were suspected of hijacking silver and merchandise pack mule trains driven by Mexican transporters and dealers who would travel across the border looking for more lucrative American markets. The brutal killings of these Mexican traffickers, (themselves of questionable repute and suspicioned to be running a smuggling enterprise across the international line), were becoming a sensitive geo-political issue between the United States and Mexican governments.

The Cowboys were also prime suspects in robberies of Wells Fargo bullion and payroll stages during that same period.

Should Wyatt have succeeded in securing the new County Sheriff's post, the Earps would have controlled law enforcement both in the city of Tombstone, and in the surrounding countryside, obviously an intolerable condition for the rustlers.

What started as a few minor harassments between the Cowboys and the Tombstone lawmen, soon developed into a struggle for control and influence of the region, which, spurred by sporadic but non-fatal clashes to date, inexorably evolved into a personal animosity....a feud....between the Earp brothers and Doc Holliday on the one side, and the Clantons and the McLaurys on the other.

A bloody confrontation awaited. Threats by the Cowboys against the Earps and Doc Holliday were common knowledge on the streets of Tombstone.

An ominous series of incidents between the two factions started in the local gambling saloons on the night of October 25, 1881. By the early afternoon of the next day, everyone who was witness to the hearsay, or to the actual scene in Tombstone, was aware that a showdown was imminent.

It came, in its most bloody and savage fury, on the afternoon of October 26, 1881, on Fremont Street, near the O.K. Corral.

JUST BEFORE THE SHOOTING STARTS

The three six-foot tall Earp brothers, Virgil, Wyatt, and Morgan, and their controversial ally, Doc Holliday, were informed that the Cowboys were armed and theatening a fight just as the hour approached 2:00 p.m. on the afternoon of October 26th.

Doc Holliday, nursing some physical discomfort on that cold afternoon, wore a long gray coat that hung below his knees. He carried a cane to steady himself. The Earp party, sporting drooping mustaches, and clothed in the dark-colored attire of the professional gamblers of that era, all carried pistols.

In addition, Virgil had just acquired a sawed-off shotgun from the Wells Fargo office on Allen Street.

When informed of the Cowboy's whereabouts on Fremont Street, the Earp group was seen massing in front of Haffords Corner on Fourth and Allen Streets.

Doc Holliday, armed with his trademark nickel-plated pistol, in a scabbard on his right hip, exchanged his cane for Virgil's sawed-off shotgun, at the behest of the Marshal himself. Virgil Earp did not think it helpful to addressing the tensions of the moment, by publicly brandishing such a sinister weapon in the streets.

With his long coat, Doc could hide the gun under his left armpit, (inside the coat), holding the weapon from the outside by his left hand down naturally at his side.

So armed, ready, and grimly determined to confront the Cowboys, the Earp brothers and Doc Holliday started on their 'walk with destiny', down Fourth Street, to turn left (west) on Fremont, and to meet their enemies.

Meanwhile, the Cowboys, comprising Ike and Billy Clanton, Tom and Frank McLaury, and newly-located cohort, Billy Claibourne, were now standing in the vacant lot next to Fly's Boarding House, in discussion with the opportunistic Sheriff John Behan about whether they should surrender their arms, in light of the impending threat to their safety attributed to the Earps and to Doc Holliday.

The Cowboys seemed divided as to their next course of action. Should they leave town, or remain only to risk a fight with the Earp party?

A drunken and garrulous Ike Clanton, up all night from a binge and confrontations with the Earp congregation, was still defiant, even though Virgil Earp had, within the past two hours, clubbed him over the head with a pistol, disarmed him, and in the company of brother Morgan, had hauled the whiskey-soddened Clanton off to the court house to be fined for carrying weapons in the streets of Tombstone.

Ike's 19-year old brother, 'Billy', packing a revolver on his hip, seemed to want to avoid trouble, and was later reported to have pressed his cantankerous older brother to leave town. Billy held the reins of his horse, now standing in the vacant lot beside him.

Frank McLaury, considered the most hostile and dangerous when armed, (as he was with a six shooter in plain sight on his hip), was testy. He told Sheriff Behan that to disarm the Cowboy group would only be acceptable if the Earps and Doc Holliday were likewise relieved of their weapons. Frank's horse, with rifle in plain view in the saddle scabbard, was standing beside him.

Tom McLaury, younger brother of the more pompous Frank, was in no temperament to want to fight. He had just had a set-to with Wyatt Earp on Fourth Street, just about 1:00 p.m. In the heated exchange, Wyatt pistol-whipped the young cowboy several times, and left him sprawled and bleeding in the street. Eyewitnesses would later testify that Tom had re-armed himself with a pistol, because they could discern the shape of such an object protruding in his right trousers pocket, when he was spotted exiting a butcher shop on Allen Street, sometime close to 2:00 p.m.

Billy 'The Kid' Claibourne did not seem committed to join in the impending battle alongside his confederates against the Earps and Holliday. He was not involved in any of the clashes between the Lawmen and the Cowboys during the previous 24 hours. He appears to have entered the O.K. Corral scene, just by a common set of circumstances, when all parties in the Cowboy group found themselves in town at the same time. However, Claibourne was to testify at a later date as an eyewitness to the shooting affray that followed.

While Sheriff Behan and the Cowboys considered the question of disarmament, (to avoid a deadly confrontation with the Earps and Doc Holliday), another eyewitness would reveal in later years, that the rustlers were 'passing around the whiskey bottle' in lively fashion among themselves.

Whether the Clantons and the McLaurys planned to fight that overcast October afternoon, one hundred and ten years ago, or, to leave town peaceably, will never be satisfactorily explained. The sad fact is that while the Cowboys were busily 'debating' matters, (and gulping fire water from the jug), their formidable adversaries were approaching, now just a minute, or two away, and counting....

Clad in their shadowy-colored dress-suits, with vests and matching dark hats, the tall, imposing Earps and the gun-throwing Doc Holliday, had already rounded the corner of Fourth and Fremont Streets; had turned left headed west; had just passed the back exit of the O.K. Corral between the Papago Cash Store and Bauer's Union Market; and were now seen approaching under the end of the awning of Bauer's, just seconds away from the Cowboys.

Sheriff Behan spotted the arriving Lawmen. Now, some of the Cowboys could see the Earps and Doc Holliday coming into view, as well. As the combatants eyed each other, getting ever closer, it must have been a most chilling realization for all to know that this was it!

Sheriff Behan left the Cowboys in the vacant lot, and hurried to meet the Earp party, to turn them away from the violent calamity that he knew was about to descend upon those who would soon face off against each other, that infamous day in Tombstone. He met the Earp brothers and Doc Holliday at the west end of Bauer's, on the sidewalk. He warned Virgil and his deputies not to "go down there", (the vacant lot) because they would be killed. But the Marshal remained steadfast in his intent to disarm the Cowboy crowd. Sheriff Behan then tried to enforce his authority as County Sheriff. He told them (Earps) to leave the scene. The Lawmen refused. Mr. Behan implied that he had the Cowboys under control and that he had demobilized their group. The Officers ignored this claim. The Marshal's party could see that Billy Clanton and Frank McLaury were wearing their pistols; that rifles were plainly visible in the saddles of the two horses; and that Tom McLaury could still have a pistol in the waistband of his pants, concealed by his vest, or, in his trouser pocket.

Ike Clanton, too, could have re-armed himself and might have been carrying a pistol under his coat. The Earp party had no way of ascertaining this from their position. Besides, the code of survival of those dangerous times, was always to assume the worst, and to expect your opponent to come out 'a'smokin'.

Wyatt Earp said it best, when he testified at his own defense during his murder trial that was to follow in Tombstone, the entire month of November, 1881. Stated Wyatt, "and I naturally kept my eyes open, for I did not intend that any of the gang should get the drop on me if I could help it".

An eyewitness, Mrs. M. King, in Bauer's Meat Market, would later report that she heard Morgan Earp tell Doc Holliday to...."Let them have it"....with Holliday answering...."All right", as the Earp party passed the door of the butcher shop enroute to face the Cowboys.

The Earp brothers and Holliday kept on going, right past an increasingly hysterical Sheriff Behan, oblivious to his exhortations for them to stop. The Marshal's party pulled their pistols as they passed in front of the entrance to Fly's Boarding House....next stop....dead ahead....the vacant lot just west of Fly's, where some of the Cowboys were now falling back against the outside wall of the Harwood building.

Seeing pistols already in the hands of Wyatt and Morgan Earp, and a nickel-plated revolver brandished by Doc Holliday, (Doc still held the sawed-off shotgun under his coat with his left hand, while he held his six-shooter with his right hand); and knowing that Virgil also carried a pistol at his waist, the Cowboys began to prepare for the worst.

Frank McLaury, now committed what some analysts would later interpret as an act of menacing bravado only, and not as a pre-meditated act of mortal combat. Frank began to drop his hand to his pistol at his side, fingering the hammer of his gun, preparing to cock the same. Frank, to Billy Clanton's left, was now partially out on Fremont Street. In fact some would say that he, (Frank), stood at the end of a sort of no man's land where the wooden sidewalk of the Harwood House met Fremont Street, but that his horse, stretching the full length of the reins, was more out on the road.

Billy Clanton, steadying his horse behind him and to his right, executed a behind-the-back maneuver that was instantly diagnosed by the Earp quartet. He began to transfer the horse's reins from his right to his left hand, thereby starting to free his gun hand to reach for the six-shooter on his right hip. At the end of this sleight-of-hand movement, Clanton's right hand was clasped solidly on the butt of his revolver, ready to pull and fire, while his left arm remained curled around behind him holding the horse.

Tom McLaury was positioned to the right of Billy Clanton. Billy's horse would actually nudge Tom, from behind, depending on how it moved its head. Otherwise the animal could, at times, conceal part, or all, of McLaury. With a rifle in the saddle scabbard, Tom was not prone to putting any distance between himself and Billy's horse, if he could help it.

Billy 'The Kid' Claibourne stood deepest inside the vacant lot toward the middle, with the O.K. Corral stalls to his rear. No weapons were visible on Claibourne.

Ike Clanton was to the far right of Tom McLaury, in the center foreground of the vacant lot, just a few feet from the west wall of Fly's Boarding House. Ike did not appear to have a sidearm or a cartridge belt around his waist. But he could have stashed a six-gun in one of the inside pockets of his coat.

As the Marshal's party came upon them, the Cowboys were now standing (from the Earp's line of sight), looking left to right, Ike Clanton....Tom McLaury....Billy Clanton....and Frank McLaury....with Billy Claibourne behind Ike and Tom deeper into the lot.

Wyatt Earp, pistol in right hand, now assumed the most inside position of his party.

He was nearest the buildings on the left (south) side of Fremont Street. He turned, left, as he got beyond the Fly's Rooming House, and walked into the lot itself, stopping but a few feet from Ike Clanton.

Virgil Earp, cane in his right hand, was to his brother Wyatt's immediate right. He too turned left into the lot, and he faced the central core of the Cowboys, with Billy Claibourne farthest away and to the rear of the lot; Tom McLaury in the middle; Billy Clanton's increasingly wary horse behind, or alongside Tom, depending on the ebb and flow of body movements in the now cramped enclosure, and with Billy himself, to the right, almost backed against the Harwood House; and Frank McLaury to the extreme right.

Morgan Earp, to Virgil's right, his pistol drawn, stood between the entrance to the vacant lot and toward the street edge of the sidewalks, looking diagonally, (leftward), back in at Billy Clanton. When he stopped, he was only about six feet from the youthful cowboy.

Doc Holliday, to Morgan's right, was further out, on Fremont Street, his nickel-plated pistol in hand, clearly visible to eyewitnesses. Doc was closest and in front of Frank McLaury. They stood facing each other, literally 'inches' between them, at first, with Doc standing to the outside of his Cowboy adversary looking back in, (leftward), muttering the most unprintable obscenities known to the language of the Frontier to that time.

Sheriff John Behan had since given up his attempts to persuade the Earp-Holliday coterie to withdraw. His entreaties for a peaceful settlement falling on deaf ears, the astutely political, but nefarious Behan now sought safe refuge in Fly's Boarding House.

Other eyewitnesses to the soon-to-be carnage had also removed themselves in the face of the encroaching hostilities. Names such as Will 'Billy' Allen....R. F. Coleman....Robert S. Hatch....and Wesley 'Wes' Fuller, (to name just a few)....were to all surface later to testify at the murder trial of the Earp brothers and Doc Holliday.

But, that comes later. What is now, is now. Nine determined and dangerous men of the Old West have come face-to-face. Most are armed, their pistols out, or in their holsters at the ready. The semi-enclosure that they find themselves standing in seems like a veritable death trap. There are scores to settle. The taunts, insults, and the humiliations hurled against each other during the past year have brought it all to the point of a showdown. To back down.... to capitulate....would be the ultimate political and personal suicide. There is now only one way to settle this.

Yet, there are still some among the antagonists, even in this eleventh hour, who had hoped that it would not come to this. But now, there is no place to run. No place to hide. At point blank range....whether by design, or by accident....there they stood.

HEATED WORDS

Morgan Earp, his pistol leveled at Billy Clanton's chest, said hotly, "You sons of bitches have been looking for a fight, now you can have it".

At the same time, Wyatt Earp, his long pistol barrel practically stuck into Ike Clanton's stomach, eye-to-eye, snorted, "You son of a bitch, you can have a fight".

Doc Holliday, his nickel-plated pistol just inches away from the belly of Frank McLaury, started to back up slowly, allowing a few feet....of 'shooting room'....between himself and the Cowboy.

Virgil Earp, the presiding Law Officer, announced, "We have come down here to disarm you and arrest you. Throw up your hands....I want your guns".

Frank McLaury's hand grasped his pistol, still holstered at his side, at the ready. Rightly or wrongly, the Marshal's party would claim to see this as a provocative act, justifying the start of their fusillade.

"Don't shoot....I don't want to fight"....cried Billy Clanton. However, the lightning reflexes of the proficient young gun-toter came into play in the face of the unmistakable threat now standing before him. Billy gripped his still-holstered pistol. (Another hostile act to be mentioned later by the Earp party.) But Billy's left arm, curled behind his back, dropped the horse's reins to the ground.

"I have nothing", stated Tom McLaury who held open his vest with both hands, as if to reveal that he was unarmed and not intending to fight. And yet, like Billy Clanton next to him, Tom was quick to react to the very real danger posed by the Earps, and Doc Holliday in front of him. Instinctively, Tom grabbed for the now loose reins of Billy's horse with his left hand. With the other hand, he continued to hold open the right side of his vest....for the moment....but, only for the moment. Tom did have 'something', in his right trousers pocket.

"Hold....I don't mean that"....pleaded Virgil, as he incredulously watched two of his own party, namely, Doc Holliday and Morgan Earp, cock their pistols to fire!

Ike Clanton, showing no weapons, edged even closer towards Wyatt Earp, to attempt to physically restrain him (Earp), from firing his pistol. Ike started to reach for Wyatt's right gun hand, in order to hold Earp's revolver away from the line of fire. At the same time, Ike reached for Wyatt's left shoulder, with his (Ike's) right hand. A struggle between both men was about to ensue.

Billy 'The Kid' Claibourne now wanted out. He half raised his hands in a gesture perceived as non-threatening, and began to bolt for the rear door of Fly's Boarding House, only steps away to his right. Claibourne's abrupt and disquieting dash for the nearest exit was all that was needed to explode the tensions in the packed enclosure, and to set off the fully cocked six-shooters of Doc Holliday and Morgan Earp. Hell was about to break loose in Tombstone.

THE SHOOTING STARTS

SHOT

DOC HOLLIDAY fires almost point blank at Frank McLaury. The bullet hits one inch left of the navel. His shirt on fire from powder burns, Frank screams, spits blood. Staggers. He is being pulled by his spooked horse, as he holds onto the reins with his left hand. He reaches again for his pistol with his right.

SHOT

MORGAN EARP fires from close range at Billy Clanton. The bullet strikes Billy two inches left of the left nipple. Billy is slammed back by the impact against his right shoulder to the Harwood House wall. Morgan has just saved older brother Virgil's life. The quick-drawing Clanton was already in the act of shooting at the Marshal standing just ten feet to his front. (Morg and Doc's firearms are the first to go off; Doc's first; Morg's second; two shots almost together; to the extent that witnesses could not seem to agree whether there were actually separate reports, or just one.)

SHOT

BILLY CLANTON simultaneously fires off a bullet that goes awry, (misses Virgil), as Morgan Earp's .45 caliber slug tears through his upper body, throwing the young Cowboy out of position.

SHOT

MORGAN EARP fires another shot, in quick succession, at Billy Clanton. Morg's bullet catches Billy on the inside of his right gun-hand, next to the thumb. The slug penetrates clear through. It shatters the wrist as it exits on the other side. But, in a remarkable display of grit and determination, Billy still manages to hang onto his weapon.

SHOT

WYATT EARP, (after four shots have been fired), accidentally discharges his pistol as Ike Clanton grabs his, (Wyatt's), shooting arm, and holds it away. This errant bullet is probably the one that skimmed the pants leg, near the knee, of Billy Claibourne, then in the act of running by the scuffling Wyatt Earp and Ike Clanton, into the back door of the Fly's hostelry. Ike starts to push Wyatt to the right, alongside the west wall of Fly's Boarding House.

A PAUSE IN THE SHOOTING

Suddenly, all guns are silent. No shooting for a few precious, eerie seconds....

Frank McLaury is being forced by his horse to the middle of Fremont Street. He still tries to clear his pistol, to shoot back at Doc Holliday, or at any of the Lawmen around him.

Plates Five & Six

"Suddenly, all guns are silent. No shooting for a few precious eerie seconds...."

Michael M. Hickey,
Street Fight in Tombstone,
Near the O.K. Corral

"....even though I was in a panic, I remember the distinct lull that occurred during the shooting. The fight might have ended with the first exchange. Ike Clanton ran. Tom McLaury had ducked behind a horse and hadn't fired yet."

Mrs. Wyatt 'Josie' Earp from
her recollections in the book
I Married Wyatt Earp
by Glenn G. Boyer

"That, there appeared to nearby listeners to be a slight pause following the opening shots, (herewith attributed to Doc Holliday; Morgan Earp; Billy Clanton; and to the accidental discharge of Wyatt's revolver), seems perfectly understandable. To shoot to kill, under such conditions, one would need to have a target. What targets could be presented if we are to try to imagine the scene following the first series of shots?....The preponderance of testimony indicates that immediately upon receiving Doc Holliday's first pistol shot to his belly, Frank McLaury, and his bucking horse, started to move out to the middle of Fremont Street, to the opposite side....That means that Morgan Earp and Doc Holliday probably jumped out of the way of the oncoming frenzied animal....This author's scenario of Frank McLaury being pulled by his horse backing out into the street, around, and past, Doc Holliday and Morgan Earp, (themselves dancing out of the way of the spooked animal), would momentarily remove McLaury as a hittable target for Doc and Morg. A pause. No shooting here."

"That, meanwhile, in the vacant lot, Wyatt Earp and Ike Clanton were engaged in a wrestling match near the northwest wall of Fly's Boarding House."

"That, Virgil Earp....was standing transfixed in stark disbelief of the horrific events around him; holding his cane in the air; and with 'the pause' then in effect, must have been hoping for dear life that the shooting would stop, then and there."

"That, Billy Claibourne was long gone, having bolted into Fly's Boarding House and away from the pandemonium."

"That, Tom McLaury, according to this author's depiction of the opening events, grabbed the reins of Billy Clanton's horse; jumped behind it; was reaching for a pistol in his right pants pocket; and was trying to control the animal by holding the saddle horn at the same time....That means that the horse had to pass in front of Billy Clanton, on its way out of the vacant lot, with Tom McLaury right along with it. For a brief pause, the younger McLaury was no target for any shooter....Tom was behind the horse...."

"That, so was the wounded Billy Clanton. He had to be protected for a few seconds by the animal as it fought its way into Fremont Street....while Billy was in the act of switching his pistol from his shattered right hand to his left, (and leaning against the Harwood wall trying to keep on his feet), he was hidden from view by the horse struggling in front of him, with Tom McLaury in control. No targets here. The pause."

Michael M. Hickey,
Street Fight in Tombstone,
Near the O.K. Corral
Excerpted from Author's
Working Notes

Virgil Earp is still holding the cane aloft, as if frozen with disbelief.

Wyatt struggles with Ike Clanton.

Doc Holliday is now suddenly on the opposite side of Frank McLaury, whose terrified horse has now heaved and kicked to a position between the two.

Morgan Earp, assuming Billy Clanton to be out of action, also finds himself on the opposite side of Frank McLaury (horse in middle). Both Doc and Morgan prepare to fire at Frank once they can get a clear shot.

Tom McLaury is now behind Billy Clanton's horse, which is panicked by the shooting and trying to break free to bolt out of the vacant lot to Fremont Street to follow Frank McLaury's horse. In so doing, Tom is hanging onto the saddle horn, and reaching for a pistol in his right pants pocket. The horse now protecting Tom, (and Billy Clanton), is restrained by Tom....but not for long....

Billy Clanton, slouching sideways on his right shoulder to the Harwood House, and with blood rushing from his left lung, and from his broken right wrist, is trying to switch his pistol to his left hand.

'Billy The Kid' Claibourne has vacated the field of battle. He has already entered the rear door of Fly's Rooming House.

THE SHOOTING STARTS AGAIN

SHOT

DOC HOLLIDAY fires at Frank McLaury behind the horse. Missed.

SHOT

MORGAN EARP fires at Frank McLaury behind the horse. Missed.

Ike Clanton slams Wyatt Earp up against the west wall of Fly's Boarding House, and runs around the Fremont Street corner of Fly's, into the front door of the building. In so doing, he has just brushed the stupefied cane-wielding Virgil Earp from behind, as he (Ike) spurts by at top speed. But the Marshal's attention is so transfixed to the apocalypse now unfolding before him that the flight of the instigator in this entire proceeding, Ike Clanton, seems unnoticed....except to Doc Holliday out on Fremont Street....

SHOT

MORGAN EARP fires again at Frank McLaury behind the bucking horse, a most difficult target to hit without destroying the animal. Missed.

SHOT

DOC HOLLIDAY fires at the fleeing Ike Clanton. Missed.

SHOT

DOC HOLLIDAY fires again at Ike's back. Missed. Clanton is already through the front door of the Fly's building, and out of immediate danger. (One of these shots may have ricocheted off the Fly's entrance into a wagon parked next door, in front of Bauer's Market.)

Tom McLaury has crossed in front of Billy Clanton. Tom holds onto the saddle horn. He is behind the horse. He has drawn his pistol. Tom is now looking over the saddle directly at Morgan Earp's shoulder. (Morgan has his back partially to Tom, firing at Frank McLaury in the middle of Fremont Street also behind a horse.)

Frank McLaury has drawn up alongside his horse's head, and has his pistol out, in his right hand, with the animal's reins in his left hand. The horse still shields him from Doc Holliday and from Morgan Earp, who are now out of his view on the other side of the horse, to his (Frank's) right.

Wyatt is now composed. He is righting himself with his pistol still in hand as he rebounds off of Fly's building, ready to join the gun-play, in earnest.

The terminally-wounded Billy Clanton, (now unprotected by Tom McLaury and horse just crossed in front of him out onto Fremont Street), begins to right himself too; has switched his pistol to his left hand; and tries to spring off the east wall of the Harwood House, so that he can open fire on Virgil Earp.

Virgil Earp still holds his cane. He is shocked that Doc and Morgan should initiate hostilities thereby contravening his demand for the Cowboys to give up their arms peaceably. It is Virgil's traditional law and order instinct that causes him to hesitate to draw his weapon, while all around him the scene is utter confusion. Acrid fumes of thick gun smoke. Bullets impacting everywhere. Horrifying screams of wounded and dying. A world gone mad.

Ike Clanton is racing from front-to-back inside Fly's Boarding House, determined to run through the rear photo gallery, out of its back door to the open yard to get to Allen Street to escape the mayhem, and to save his skin. Ike is terrified at the two near-misses just fired at him by

Doc Holliday. He reaches the back door of the rooming house and jerks open the door.

Morgan Earp, previously occupied with trying to hit Frank McLaury behind his (Frank's) horse, in the middle of Fremont Street, now begins to sense another horse behind him. (Tom McLaury, with drawn pistol, is aiming over the saddle of Billy Clanton's horse at Morgan Earp.)

THE COWBOYS HAVE NOT YET FIRED WITH EFFECT. THEY ARE NOW IN POSITION TO DO SO. THE SHOOTING STARTS TO BECOME GENERAL

SHOT

WYATT EARP, as quick as a cat; whirls leftward; swings his right arm holding his .45 Colt 'Peacemaker' revolver around the front of his upper body and fires a shot past his left shoulder at the source of a 'distraction' behind him. The bullet crashes into the northwest corner of the Photo Shack just behind, (south), of the main Fly's Boarding House. (In court testimony later, Ike Clanton will accuse the Earps and Doc Holliday of trying to kill him as he reported 'near misses' to his person at the Fremont Street entrance to the rooming house, and again, at the doorway to the photography gallery, as he fled through both openings enroute to freedom.) Before Wyatt can cut loose, again, toward the commotion between the two Fly's buildings, he is compelled to turn back to his right, at the nearby explosion of a pistol shot from behind a horse.

SHOT

TOM McLAURY has just fired over the horse's saddle at Morgan Earp. The horse bucks. McLaury's aim is suspect. He holds the horse in place by hanging onto the saddle horn with his left hand, his pistol in his right. Cocks to fire again, in a split second....

Wyatt Earp has just reeled back to the right toward Tom McLaury's pistol-shot noise. Spots Tom shooting at brother Morgan....Wyatt cocks his Colt single action six-shooter to fire.

Morgan Earp, with Tom McLaury's bullet whistling by him, now tries to turn completely around to face McLaury.

Doc Holliday, starting to uplift the shotgun from beneath the left side of his overcoat, is now half-twirling, to accost Tom McLaury, too.

Virgil, sensing mortal danger to brother Morgan, now switches the cane

The Wounding of Morgan Earp.

Plates Seven & Eight

"I'm hit", groans MORGAN EARP, as he begins to twist and topple backward on Fremont Street, having just taken a bullet in his right shoulder, which will rip across the width of his back and exit out the left. Morg will rise up immediately and continue shooting.

TOM McLAURY, firing over the saddle of Billy Clanton's horse, is Morgan's attacker. McLaury has just shot twice in the deadly Tombstone showdown, after managing to maneuver with the horse past the wounded Billy Clanton, and right out of the death trap-like vacant lot to his vantage point, as depicted here by Master Artist and Illustrator, Bruce R. Greene. But Tom has just had his one last fleeting moment of glory....

WYATT EARP, in a blind rage at seeing younger favorite brother Morgan come under such close-range assault, will snap two back-to-back retaliatory shots at Tom McLaury from

within the vacant lot, both just missing the Cowboy, but the first of which will char the mane of Tom's horse, causing the pain-inflicted animal to bolt uncontrollably out of Tom's grasp. Wyatt's first shot is shown here.

And DOC HOLLIDAY will be waiting. Standing out on Fremont Street, preparing to blast a load of lethal buckshot, point blank, at the approaching McLaury, Doc is seen here unfolding the sawed-off double barreled shotgun from beneath the left side of his long gray coat. At the same time, the switch-hitting Holliday is holstering his short snouted nickel-plated Colt pistol in its scabbard, high up on his right hip under the overcoat, after just having fired with it at Ike Clanton, who has escaped the bedlam by running through the front door of the Fly's house.

Ike's game teenage brother, BILLY CLANTON, has momentarily regrouped from the two pistol shots fired into him by Morgan Earp during the opening seconds of the historic street battle. Billy is seen here leaning on his right shoulder against the Harwood House. He has just changed his six-shooter from his shattered gun hand to his left. Despite also absorbing a .45 caliber slug directly into his left lung, the courageous 19-year old Cowboy still manages to open fire on Virgil Earp, standing opposite, with his back to the street-side corner of the Fly's building. Clanton's shot is wild.

Tombstone City Marshal, VIRGIL EARP, is finally jolted from his disbelieving stupor at seeing the Fremont Street confrontation now completely out of control, as the direct result of the homicidal start-up fire of Doc Holliday and Morgan Earp against Frank McLaury and Billy Clanton, respectively. Having brandished a cane up to this point, (instead of initially drawing his revolver to join the fighting), the Marshal has now moved the stick to his left hand, and jerked his gun with his right, at the heart-wrenching sight of his brother Morgan being 'dropped to the street' by the bullet to the shoulder, just fired by Tom McLaury.

But Virgil is unaware of the menacing presence of the critically wounded, but still ever-dangerous FRANK McLAURY, who has now yanked his sidearm, yet all the while hanging onto the reins of his horse with his left hand, toward the opposite, (north), side of the road. The fast-shooting Frank is about to unload his own barrage of bullets into the vacant lot from under the neck of his horse, the first of which will almost knock the Marshal off his feet, as it cuts into his lower right leg calf.

In giving her account of the blazing street fight to a Kansas City newspaper, an eye-witness, a Mrs. J. C. Colyer, was to report, "....the Cowboys opened fire on them, (Earps-Holliday), and you never saw such shooting....Another used his horse as a barricade and shot under its neck...." It is the carefully considered opinion of this author that onlooker, Mrs. Colyer, had been a first-hand witness to Frank McLaury's use of his horse as a sort of breastwork, to fire under its neck at the Earp party, from the other side of Fremont Street.

to his left hand. Draws his pistol with his right.

Billy Clanton raises his pistol in his left hand to fire at Virgil.

Ike Clanton is now out of the immediate area of the shooting.

SHOT **BILLY CLANTON** fires wildly at Virgil Earp. Billy's shot goes astray.

SHOT **TOM McLAURY**, with lightning speed, fires again at Morgan's back. Hit. The slug catches Morgan in the initial act of a rightward turn-around. Tom's bullet enters Morgan's right shoulder, tears across the back, exiting the left shoulder. Morgan starts to topple backwards.

SHOT **WYATT EARP** 'lets go' a bullet at Tom McLaury, enraged at the sight of his favorite brother Morgan being felled by the shot in the back! But the horse still conceals Tom. Yet, Wyatt's bullet zings the horse's mane. The smell of smoke and flecks of gun powder on the horse's hair. The animal starts to heave and to tug at its reins. It is out of control, dragging Tom further out to the street. Tom is forced to let go of the saddle horn. With his just-freed left hand he starts to grab for the rifle scabbard as a last resort, to control the horse between him and the Earp party. Tom still has his pistol in his right hand, but he cannot fire, due to the frenzied horse.

Morgan Earp yells...."I'm hit", as he falls backward and lands on the street, from Tom McLaury's just-fired bullet.

Frank McLaury holds his horse's head with his left hand gripping the shortened reins. He bends down under the horse's neck, aims his pistol in the direction of Virgil and Wyatt, to his front.

Virgil Earp now has his pistol out, to respond to Billy Clanton's attack. He is distracted momentarily by brother Morgan's collapse on the street, to his right. He does not see Frank McLaury taking aim in his direction from under the horse's neck from out in the middle of Fremont Street.

Billy Clanton tries tediously to re-cock his revolver to continue his assault on the Marshal. His crippled six-foot frame keeps causing his legs to contort and to fold under the massive weight of his body. Each time he rights himself, he slides toward the Fremont Street corner of the Harwood House.

Wyatt Earp, still maddened by the shooting of brother Morgan, takes aim again, to try to finish Tom McLaury, even if it means destroying the

THE WOUNDING OF VIRGIL EARP

Death of Tom McLaury.

Plates Nine & Ten

KA BOOM, thunders the sawed-off shotgun just fired by DOC HOLLIDAY, almost face-to-face at TOM McLAURY, who is seen taking the salvo of buckshot in his ribs on the right side of his body. Doc got his chance to attack McLaury when the Cowboy's horse finally freed itself and raced out of the vacant lot, exposing Tom to Holliday's earth-shaking blast. Tom's strength and determination to remain on his feet despite the twelve clusters of shrapnel in his rib cage, is equally startling. The game cattle rancher-rustler will still manage to stagger away from Holliday and the shoot-out scene to the Third Street corner, (to the right and outside of this illustration), where he will eventually collapse. McLaury's hat is jolted from his head by the force of the shotgun broadside, revealing the bandages believed administered earlier that afternoon when Tom sought treatment for wounds near his left temple, brought on by a pistol whipping from Wyatt Earp in a brief altercation on Fourth Street, about an hour before the fight.

WYATT EARP is still not finished with Tom. Earp is believed, by the author, to have fired twice at McLaury during the thirty second gun battle on October 26, 1881. The first shot, when Tom was behind the horse, missed the Cowboy, but grazed the animal causing it to panic and to break away. Wyatt's second attempt, (at the very same moment that Earp loyalist, Doc Holliday, 'cuts loose' with the shotgun), barely misses McLaury too. It is depicted here, and shows Earp standing erect, inside of the vacant lot with his back to Fly's Boarding House, in the act of shooting, "as cool as a cucumber", as Wyatt was described by eyewitness, R. F. Coleman, in the feature story about the Frontier showdown that appeared in the Tombstone Epitaph newspaper the following day, October 27th.

Across from Wyatt, leaning on his right shoulder against the Harwood House corner, is BILLY CLANTON, who has now successfully switched his six-gun from his crippled right hand to his left. With a seemingly super-human effort, the youthful Clanton still manages to shoot with his non-gun hand, albeit wildly, at Marshal Virgil Earp, directly opposite near the street edge of the main Fly's house. Billy's revolver is shown by Master Artist and Illustrator, Bruce R. Greene, in upward recoil, from the exploding .45 caliber bullet he has just 'snapped' at the Marshal.

VIRGIL EARP, himself, seems to be stumbling, his right foot slightly raised, as he tries to remain standing. Virgil had transferred the cane to his left hand, and finally pulled his Colt .45 long snouted six shooter to join the fighting when he saw his younger brother, Morgan, take a close-in 'shoulder hit' from Tom McLaury, the Cowboy shooting from over the saddle of the horse. Virgil has just been hit in the right leg calf. The bullet has passed cleanly through the flesh without touching the shin bone. Which explains why the Marshal is off balance and looking downward, even as he starts to come under attack from Billy Clanton.

MORGAN EARP has just fallen to the ground after taking Tom McLaury's bullet across his back. But the hot-blooded Morg is still firmly in control of his pistol. He will spring back up from the street, immediately, to rejoin the deadly hostilities.

FRANK McLAURY is Virgil's assailant. The most feared of the Cowboy gunmen, the gut-shot McLaury has regrouped, and has maneuvered with his horse almost to the other side, (north), of Fremont Street, where he still grips the animal's reins with his left hand. With revolver now drawn in his right hand, Frank has just fired his first shot in the violent Tombstone fracas from under the neck of his horse, the .45 caliber bullet almost knocking the Marshal off his feet. But the deafening fire from Doc Holliday's sawed-off shotgun nearby, and from Frank's own lead-spewing weapon, will prove to be too much for the already terrorized animal. It is about to pull away and gallop for its life down Fremont Street, to the left and outside of this picture. Without the horse to protect him, Frank will have only minutes to live. He will come under instant rapid fire pursuit from Doc Holliday and Morgan Earp in the street, and from Wyatt Earp shooting from within the vacant lot. The fight will end after this.

terror-stricken animal hiding him.

Doc Holliday's attention is now inextricably directed at the 'screeching' horse dragging Tom McLaury in his, (Doc's), direction. At the same time, Tom is being gradually thrown outward straight at Holliday, by the spinning horse. The horse now breaks away. Tom is aghast at the sight of that sawed-off shotgun! Tom raises his right arm to shield his face, pistol in hand, not able to fire as he tries to keep his balance and remain upright on his feet....to escape the wrath of Doc Holliday.

SHOT

FRANK McLAURY fires from under his horse, crouching, almost reaching around the horse's front, (under neck), with his right gun hand, while he steadies the horse with his left hand. Hit. The bullet strikes Virgil Earp in the fleshy part of his right calf and passes through the leg. Earp stumbles. He is almost knocked off his feet by the force of the projectile. Steadies himself immediately to a position facing his assailant, the bent over, wounded, but still dangerous, Frank McLaury.

SHOTGUN

DOC HOLLIDAY, at the same time, discharges one burst into the exposed right rib cage of Tom McLaury, almost at point blank range, under McLaury's raised right arm....twelve buckshot wounds, within the diameter of a flattened palm of a man's hand. Tom is rocked back by the percussion, lurching wildly away from Holliday, toward the corner of Fremont and Third Streets.

SHOT

WYATT EARP shoots again at Tom McLaury at the very moment that Tom receives Doc Holliday's load of shotgun shrapnel. Wyatt misses. But it matters little. McLaury is practically dead on his feet.

Tom McLaury, oozing blood all over the street from the exploding charges of Doc's shotgun, is still clutching his pistol. But, Tom can no longer threaten anyone. He now appears, to eyewitnesses, to be running away from Doc Holliday and from the scene of the shoot-out.

SHOT

VIRGIL EARP returns fire (one shot), at Frank McLaury behind the horse. Missed. But the bullet may have grazed the horse.

SHOTGUN

DOC HOLLIDAY 'lets loose' the other load of buckshot at the rapidly fleeing, (but already dying), Tom McLaury, as Doc is not certain Tom is finished. The shotgun burst is meaningless. Amazingly, McLaury has already put too much distance between himself and his assailant. Doc, in disgust, throws the weapon aside, and again, reaches for his nickel-plated pistol.

SHOT

FRANK McLAURY fires again in the direction of Virgil and Wyatt Earp, (the latter who had just fired, and missed, at brother Tom). Frank's shot is wild. The last series of shots at, or near, Frank McLaury, including Doc's intimidating shotgun blasts, has finally unnerved Frank's horse. The injured Frank, traumatized from his belly wound and fatal loss of blood, is now losing his left-hand hold of the horse's reins. The animal begins to pull away, heading east toward Fourth Street, at a gallop. Frank is only a split second away from being exposed, in the middle of Fremont Street, to an enfilade from the Earp party. Wyatt takes immediate notice and shifts his attention to Frank McLaury.

SHOT

BILLY CLANTON fires at Virgil Earp. Missed. With gun hand, (right), shattered earlier by Morgan Earp's bullet, Billy can just barely raise his pistol with his left. Fatally wounded in his chest, he is still leaning against the outside wall of the Harwood House, trying to prop himself erect at the same time. When he reaches forward with his left arm to aim at Virgil, simultaneously supporting his shooting hand with his crippled raised right fist, he automatically exposes his right side to return fire from Virgil, now opposite. (Virgil himself, just fired back at Frank McLaury. The Marshal now swings back, leftward, to face his latest attacker, the youngest and the gamest of the Clantons.)

SHOT

VIRGIL EARP answers Billy Clanton shot-for-shot. In fact, Virgil will fire his last three shots at Billy. This first bullet hits Clanton six inches right of the navel, below the twelfth rib on the right side of the body. Billy is flattened squarely against the Harwood House. He sinks rapidly to the ground, his legs giving out in front of him. But his downward slide is interrupted. It appears that he has caught the shirt sleeve of his left hand on part of the house behind him. His re-cocked six-shooter is momentarily useless. It is suspended above his head. Clanton twists and turns to free himself, aware that Marshal Earp must be taking aim at him, again.

SHOT

BILLY CLANTON, the sheer weight of his six-foot bulk dragging him downward, lands on his rump, legs spread-eagled in front of him, his back against the corner of the Harwood building. As his left gun-hand pulls free above his head, his pistol discharges in the air toward Virgil. Missed.

SHOT

VIRGIL EARP, now thumbing salvo after salvo, fires back at Billy Clanton. Missed. Bullet hits the wall above the head of Clanton, who, had he not just slid down the outside of the Harwood building, would have probably taken another direct hit from the Marshal.

Tom McLaury has already collapsed at the corner of Third and Fremont Streets. He is unable to speak. His pistol is on the ground by his side. Full of shotgun pellets, he is breathing his last.

Billy Clanton, still determined to exact a toll on the Earps, is in the act of cocking his pistol again, lying in a pool of his own blood. Losing strength by the second, he rests his weapon on his knees and prepares to fire.

Frank McLaury is weaving around on Fremont Street, almost directly opposite of Fly's Rooming House. His pistol is in his right hand. His left hand is clutching his profusely-bleeding abdomen. Having just lost control of the reins of his horse which is now in the process of racing toward Fourth Street, Frank is vulnerable to attack from Doc Holliday to his right; Morgan Earp, also to his right, but now raising himself up again from the ground; and, from Wyatt, also diagonally to his right, inside the vacant lot.

Doc Holliday, now re-armed with his nickel-plated pistol, starts to turn from the dying Tom McLaury, (to the west), leftward back to the shoot-out enclosure in the vacant lot next to Fly's Rooming House, where Virgil Earp and Billy Clanton are in the act of exchanging a withering staccato of fire. But suddenly, Doc feels the portentous stare of Frank McLaury behind his right shoulder. Holliday halts in mid-turn. Swivels back in the other direction, (clockwise), and ends up offering his bean pole-like right side silhouette to Frank. At that precise moment, the visibly shakened McLaury must realize that this is his last chance to make it all count. He un-clutches his blooding navel. Raises his left arm to 'cock it', chest high, into an L-shape across his upper body. Using the forearm as support, he steadies his right gun hand on it. Frank laboriously pulls back the hammer of his .45 Colt revolver, to fire the shot that he hopes will take Doc Holliday to the Gates of Hell....

Morgan Earp is now back on his feet. He crouches next to Doc Holliday. With bloodied shoulders, Morg determinedly starts to cock his pistol to address the viperous threat in the form of the just-horseless Frank McLaury, the latter now inclining in an easterly direction along Fremont Street.

Wyatt Earp intends his last shot for the most skilled of the Cowboy shootists, Frank McLaury. Wyatt prepares to fire now that McLaury is free of the horse, is without cover, out in the open, and still a very real danger to his younger brother, and to his most loyal and trusted friend, Doc Holliday.

Virgil Earp is in the act of cocking his pistol to shoot back at Billy Clanton.

TWENTY FIVE SECONDS ESTIMATED SINCE THE START OF SHOOTING.
NOW BEGINS THE FINAL FIVE SECONDS

SHOT

BILLY CLANTON fires at Virgil Earp. Missed. Billy can no longer aim effectively, even when he steadies his hands by holding his pistol on his knees. He has sustained three wounds, two of which are fatal. Gamely, he wants to cock his pistol, again. But the young Cowboy has just fired the last shot of his life.

SHOT

VIRGIL EARP fires at Billy Clanton. (The two shots are practically as one.) Virgil's bullet perforates Billy's trousers leg near the right knee, but does not touch the flesh. The pants cloth starts to smolder from the effects of the powder burns. While at that exact same moment out in the middle of Fremont Street....

"I've got you now", says Frank McLaury to Doc Holliday, as Frank is in the act of shooting Doc, literally, in the back.

"You're a good one if you have", says Doc Holliday at Frank McLaury, with Doc now having turned his head and pistol aim rightward, thereby presenting Frank with a right-to-left target of his (Doc's) back.

Wyatt Earp has taken aim at Frank McLaury that very second.

Morgan Earp has taken aim at Frank McLaury that very second.

Four guns thunder with a deafening roar, almost together.

SHOT

FRANK McLAURY fires at Doc Holliday. The bullet perforates Doc's coat pocket at the back, running practically the width of the coat. The slug hits Doc's pistol holster. This impact breaks the force of the projectile, preventing penetration of the skin behind the holster. However, a two-inch 'burn' along Doc's hip is inflicted as the bullet exits on the left side of Doc's coat.

"I'm shot right through"....eyewitnesses will later report Doc as exclaiming. The wound will prove to be superficial only.

SHOT

WYATT EARP fires and misses at Frank McLaury from the greatest distance separating these four pistoleers. Earp shoots from within the vacant lot. In so doing, his bullet sails right between brother Virgil and Billy Clanton, these latter two in the final curtain of their own life-or-death shoot-out.

SHOT

DOC HOLLIDAY fires at Frank McLaury. Missed. Doc's shot is astray because McLaury had just creased Holliday's hip with the slug that caroomed off of the pistol scabbard, jerking Holliday out of position.

SHOT

MORGAN EARP fires at Frank McLaury. Hit. Morg's bullet explodes into Frank's brain, entering just below the right ear. The jolt almost somersaults McLaury over on his head. He crashes violently to the street, pistol flying out of his right hand, quivering in shock, unable to speak a word.

"I got him"....Morgan is overheard to boast, by eyewitnesses.

THE SHOOTING STOPS

Doc Holliday runs up to the gasping Frank McLaury, pistol in hand, threatening to kill Frank. To quote Holliday, "The son of a bitch has shot me and I mean to kill him". Seeing that McLaury is already past any hope, Doc eventually withdraws to his room in Fly's Boarding House, after some post-gunfight talk on Fremont Street with Wyatt Earp and Wells Fargo undercover agent, Fred Dodge. Doc's woman, 'Big Nosed' Kate Elder, reported some time later that Doc seemed distraught and repentant by the day's events. Doc Holliday was to ultimately submit to the creeping tuberculosis that seemed to have plagued him all of his adult life. He died in bed, in Glenwood Springs, Colorado, in November, 1887, at age 36.

Billy Clanton, the breath of life seeping from him, is still trying to cock his pistol when C. S. Fly, (with rifle), runs out of his house, and with Robert S. Hatch as witness, takes the pistol out of Billy's hand. Billy asks for more cartridges. The young Cowboy is carried into the building, on the other side of the Harwood House, at the street corner of Fremont and Third. His boots are removed. Shirt and trousers loosened. He is made as comfortable as possible. Billy is in extreme pain. He is heard to exclaim loudly that he was murdered. He demands that the crowd clear the doorway so he can die peacefully. He asks for something to put him to sleep. He dies within the hour. His empty pistol is retrieved by the coroner, H. M. Mathews.

Plates Eleven & Twelve

"I looked and saw him, (Frank McLaury), running and a shot was fired and he fell over on his head....I heard Morg Earp say, 'I got him'. There may have been a couple of shots afterward, but that was the end of the fight."

Sheriff John H. Behan,
Eyewitness

"....saw Doc Holliday and a man that had been pointed out to me as Frank McLaury, near the middle of Fremont Street....Frank McLaury made some remark like this; 'I have got you this time'; Holliday made some remark, 'You are a good one if you have', or words to that effect; McLaury seemed to be retreating across the street, to the opposite side of the street;....he, (McLaury), stopped and stood with his pistol across his arm, the pistol in his

right hand and resting on his left arm, and in the act of shooting; about that time I saw Doc Holliday and Morgan Earp shooting in the direction of McLaury, or at him; Frank McLaury fell to the ground at that time, as if he had been shot; the shooting seemed to be over at that time....Billy Clanton seemed to be in the act of trying to cock it, (pistol), but did not seem to have the strength to do so. (Mr.) Fly reached down and took hold of the pistol and pulled it out of his hand. As he did so, Billy Clanton said, 'give me some more cartridges'."

Robert S. Hatch, Saloon Keeper
Eyewitness

"I saw Doc Holliday in the middle of the street; the youngest of the Earp brothers, (Morgan), was about three feet from the sidewalk; he was firing at a man, (Frank McLaury), behind a horse; Holliday also fired at the man behind the horse....then I saw the man who had the horse let go, and was staggering all the time until he fell; he had his pistol still when he fell."

Mr. B. H. Fallehy, Laundryman
Eyewitness

"Billy, (Clanton), and Frank, (McLaury), both mortally wounded, still showed grit, but couldn't shoot straight anymore....After that Virge, (Earp), finished off Billy. Morg, (Earp), who had been knocked down but risen right up to continue the fight, or perhaps Wyatt, (Earp), or Doc, (Holliday), put the finishing shot into Frank, who was still on his feet, faced off in the road with Doc. Frank's last shot hit Doc in the left hip, but his pistol holster deflected it; he got only a bruise. Morg thought his shot finished Frank. Doc thought his did. Wyatt fired also, but was non-committal on the subject."

Mrs. Wyatt 'Josie' Earp from
her recollections in the book
I Married Wyatt Earp
by Glenn G. Boyer

"Frank McLaury was not exactly running but he was getting around lively when he was shot the last time. He was inclining away from the Earp party. I do not know how many times he was shot. I saw wounds on his person; one on the head; one on the belly....Doc Holliday, after the first shots were fired, was shooting at Frank McLaury on the street....Wyatt Earp was shooting at Frank McLaury....Frank McLaury separated from his horse nearby in the middle of the street....When I saw him last he was on the opposite side of the street, bent over this way, (illustrating). This was during or near the last part of the shooting."

William F. 'Billy The Kid' Claibourne,
Momentary Participant in the
Street Fight and Eyewitness

"I examined Billy Clanton; he was shot through the right wrist; his arm was broken right there....He was shot on the left side of the body; he was shot below the left nipple and the lungs were oozing out of the wound; he was shot through the pants on the right leg above the boot; did not touch the skin....My attention was drawn to a man, (Tom McLaury), dying but not dead laying alongside of the house, on the corner of Third and Fremont Streets....I asked him if he had anything to say before he died; he made us no answer; he could not speak....Don't know who it was that assisted me in carrying Tom McLaury into the house. When I got to Tom McLaury there were four or five persons about him."

Thomas Keefe, Carpenter
Eyewitness

"After the shooting was over I saw Billy Clanton lying at the end of the next house, (Harwood), below Fly's gallery....I saw he was shot twice, one in the belly about here, (above and to the right of the navel), and another shot below the left nipple. I told him he couldn't live."

Wesley 'Wes' Fuller, Jeweler
Eyewitness

Author's Note:

After Frank McLaury's spooked horse tore itself free and galloped away from its handler in an easterly direction, (to the left and outside of the picture), Frank came under instant rapid fire onslaught from Doc Holliday and Morgan and Wyatt Earp. Here is McLaury, to the extreme left, taking a fatal hit near the right ear, the fight-ending bullet just unleashed from Morgan Earp's .45 caliber pistol, as Morg crouches next to Doc Holliday on Fremont Street. The youngest of 'The Fighting Earps', that day, has still managed to shoot with hellish effect despite being felled only seconds earlier by a shoulder hit from Tom McLaury, firing over the saddle of the horse. Tom has already collapsed on the corner of Third and Fremont Streets, (to the right, and outside of the picture), having been 'blasted' at close range by Doc Holliday touting a sawed-off shotgun. The insidious double-barreled weapon is seen on the ground. It was promptly discarded by Doc, who again, pulled his short-snouted nickel-plated six shooter to face off against Frank McLaury across the street. Holliday's shot missed. Frank's did not. The Cowboy's just-fired bullet shredded the back of Doc's gray coat, entering from the right side and leaving a two inch gash on Holliday's left hip as the slug exited. An eyewitness was to hear Doc moan, "I'm shot right through", as the result of Frank's near deadly shooting. Meanwhile, from deep within the vacant lot, Wyatt Earp has also just fired at Frank McLaury, barely missing. Wyatt's bullet sails right between older brother Virgil and Billy Clanton, the latter seen lying on the ground at the corner of the Harwood House.

Virgil and Billy are in the final throes of their own life and death shoot-out, the Marshal's bullet creasing Clanton's right pants leg above the boot. Billy, using his knees for support, has fired his last shot, after sliding to the ground from the effects of three already inflicted wounds, to his left lung, right wrist, and right side of the navel underneath the twelfth rib. Tombstone Probate Court Judge and eyewitness, J. H. Lucas testified later, "I think his (Billy Clanton's) pistol was discharged twice from the time I thought he was hit till he was down on the ground....He continued to struggle until he got clear down on the ground. About the time he got to the ground, the firing ceased...."

Frank McLaury is but a few minutes from breathing his last on Fremont Street. By the time he is carried into another house across from where Billy Clanton, and his younger brother, Tom, are taken to die, Frank has passed on. His pistol is also retrieved by the coroner, Mathews. It has two un-fired cartridges in the chamber.

Tom McLaury is carried into the same house as Billy Clanton. His last breath is at hand. In shock. Eyes still open. Speechless. He expires almost immediately. But, Tom McLaury's pistol is missing! Someone removed it before the crowd started to gather at the shoot-out scene. This provoked subsequent strong anti-Earp sentiment in Tombstone, that Tom was unarmed at the time of the gunfight, and was, in fact, murdered. (Pro-Earp scholars today will insist that Sheriff Behan, himself, one of the first on the scene when the shooting stopped, took McLaury's pistol and hid it, in order to bring discredit to the Earps and to Doc Holliday.)

Wyatt Earp is unscathed. He has already re-loaded his pistol. He checks his injured brothers and has ensured their protection, and their transport with armed escorts, to their homes.

Morgan Earp, with painful shoulder wound, is carried onto an open buckboard and manually hauled by miners and supportive citizens to his home on Fremont and First Streets. Morg will recover. However, the Cowboys were to have the last word on the subject of Morgan Earp's continued presence in Tombstone following the historic Fremont Street confrontation. Almost five months later, on the evening of Saturday, March 18, 1882, shots fired from the darkness outside and through the rear door of Bob Hatch's Saloon and Billiard Parlor found their tragic mark. The well-liked, dare devil Morg, favored brother of Wyatt, and carousing comrade of Doc Holliday, was hit in the back by an assassin's bullet that shattered his spinal column, as he was playing a game of pool. Morgan died within the hour.

Virgil Earp, with a nasty leg wound, is assisted, too, onto a buckboard and pulled home by townsfolk in front of the wagon carrying his younger brother, Morgan. Destination is to the same Fremont and First Street house. Virgil's wife, Alvira (Allie), is at his side. The Marshal will be up and around and walking the Tombstone streets again by mid-December. But not for long. On the evening of December 28, 1881, Virgil was attacked while crossing Fifth Street, from the Oriental to the Crystal Palace Saloons, by shotgun-wielding ambushers firing across Allen Street. The Marshal was hit on his left side. He sustained severe wounds to his arm, particularly to the elbow area and to his back. Virgil would never regain the full use of his left arm again. He

AND THERE SHALL BE NO FINAL CHAPTER....

Wyatt Earp and Josephine Sarah Marcus
Just After the Street Fight.

Plate Thirteen

When Wyatt Earp and Josephine Sarah 'Josie' Marcus were formally introduced to each other in Tombstone in 1880, it was, as they say, love at first sight. As it often seems with such great romances, theirs was to be a forbidden love, at first, especially in the context of the so-called high moral code and societal upstanding attributed to someone of Wyatt Earp's stature in the community. For he was already living with Cecilia Ann 'Mattie' Blaylock, then accepted and held in affection by everyone in the area, as his second wife, although no official record of such a marriage has ever been uncovered by Frontier researchers. Josephine too, was not without her own encumbrance. She was betrothed, and sharing a house at the time, with none other than John H. Behan, the dapper, but slippery, later-to-be appointed Cochise County Sheriff, who was to play center stage as the arch rival and nemesis to Wyatt Earp throughout the Tombstone saga. But, despite their ties to others at the time, once Wyatt and Josie 'locked eyes', it became a foregone conclusion that the deep swirls of infatuation, and then of passion each coveted for the other, could not be long suppressed. By the time of the famous gun fight on October 26, 1881, Wyatt Earp and Josephine Sarah Marcus were a couple. And all of Tombstone knew it. That there was, and still is, the most vehement public condemnation against Wyatt for his abandonment of Mattie for Josie, (which desertion is blamed for Mattie's tragic suicide in Pinal, Arizona in July of 1888), seemed to be of little foreboding to the star-crossed, Wyatt and Josie. Their paths were now set, inexorably onward and together, for the rest of their days on earth.

Wyatt Earp was the well-known 33-year old, six foot tall, darkly clad, and handsome law man, pistoleer, gambler, and mining speculator. Josephine Sarah Marcus, barely 20 years old, from a middle-class Jewish family in San Francisco, had travelled to Tombstone initially as a nightclub stage performer. She was then in full bloom, petite but buxom, with dark eyes and long flowing hair. Her look spelled desire. The businessman and the show girl. It all made for the most lively fireside gossip amidst the fluttery 'sinless better class' of Tombstone society.

At least six inches shorter than her man, Josie looked up at Wyatt adoringly. She was young, impressionable, and adventurous, in a time of stalking danger everywhere. Life could be so fleeting in those rip-roaring days. There were no tomorrows. She was in love. She wanted him. Her ardent suitor....her knight in shining armor....her lover....hero....protector....she would have him. Public be damned. Wyatt Earp would belong to her.

About the Fremont Street fight, here is some of what Josie had to say, as recorded by premier Earp historian, Glenn G. Boyer, in his absorbing work, I Married Wyatt Earp...."I jumped up as I heard the firing start. I knew in my heart it could be only one thing. A picture flashed through my mind of Wyatt falling before the gunfire of Johnny's, (Behan), horrible poker-playing cronies....I didn't know at the time who was wounded and was too frightened to get closer. I almost swooned when I saw Wyatt's tall figure very much alive....He spotted me, ...and like a feather-brained girl, my only thought was, 'my God, I haven't got a bonnet on. What will they think?' But you can imagine my real relief at seeing my love alive. I was simply a little hysterical. Can you blame me?"

Wyatt Earp was to live on, for almost fifty years from that 'Day of Infamy' in Tombstone. He died in Los Angeles in the arms of his adulating wife in January, 1929, just two months before his 81st birthday. Josie would not re-marry. She joined her beloved Wyatt in death in 1944, in the 83rd year of her life. Today, these two storied lovers of the Old West lay interred, side by side, in the cemetery, appropriately named, 'The Hills of Eternity', in Colma, California, less than an hours drive from San Francisco.

Eternity? Yes. For it can be said of Wyatt and Josie Earp that theirs was a most tumultuous affair.

And there shall be no final chapter....

left Tombstone forever, accompanying brother Morgan's body to the family homestead in Colton, California, a few days after Morg was murdered in March, 1882. Virgil lived on, a semi-cripple, until he died peacefully in 1905, in the sixty-second year of his life.

Wyatt talks with Fred Dodge, Doc Holliday, and others, on Fremont Street following the shoot-out. Sees his mistress, Josephine Sarah 'Josie' Marcus, who had run up to the site of the gun fire, and crosses the street to meet her to assuage her fears. The look between them says it all. Upon intimation by Sheriff John Behan that he (Wyatt) would be subject to arrest for the deaths of Billy Clanton and Tom and Frank McLaury, Wyatt menaces Behan with defiant words, and coldly refuses to submit to any arrest by him, (Behan), or his party. "If you were God Almighty, you could not arrest me this day", Wyatt is reported to have said to the Sheriff, (or words to such effect), according to Fred Dodge and to another man who witnessed the dramatic exchange between the two rivals. Wyatt then visits his two wounded brothers to alert them of Behan's intentions to arrest them, and of the necessity to stand firm, and to resist, should such action be attempted. And it was to be left to Wyatt Earp to outlive all of the players in that violent Tombstone drama. He would pass on from natural causes, in bed in his Los Angeles home, just two months before his eighty-first birthday, in the year 1929.

Ike Clanton is safe and unharmed in the Emmanuel's building on Toughnut Street. But, as they say...."You can never break the mold". For Ike Clanton would continue to skirt the law until it became just a question of time before the long tireless arm of civil authority and of encroaching civilization would envelop the cattle rustler, and consign him to the Arizona desert cactus. He was shot down and killed on June 1, 1887, by Detective J. V. Brighton, in the company of Deputy Sheriff Miller, both lawmen in possession of a warrant against Clanton that they were attempting to serve at the time.

Billy 'The Kid' Claibourne is also safe and under protection of Sheriff J. H. Behan and his deputies. That is, only until the early morning of November 14th of the following year, (1882), when 'The Kid', staggering drunk, made the mistake of picking a quarrel with 'Buckskin' Frank Leslie, a Tombstone bartender by popular regard, but also an accomplished man-killer, with the speed and skills to hold his own in any gun-play. Having been forewarned by sympathetic bystanders, 'Buckskin' Frank stealthily stepped out of a side door to the Oriental Saloon, (his place of employment), to look for Claibourne, who, as expected, was laying in wait on Allen Street to catapult the multi-talented barman into the after-life. Leslie's gun spoke the more decisively. When the smoke cleared, the so-called 'Billy The Kid' Claibourne was in his last throes from a fatal gunshot wound in the side.

AUTHOR'S SELECTED INDEX AND REFERENCES

(Sworn Courtroom Testimony; Eyewitness Reports; Excerpts from
Credible Publications; and Newspaper Accounts)

October 30, 1881

Excerpt from news article in <u>The Daily Nugget</u> (newspaper), Tombstone, Arizona.

"Yesterday warrants for the arrest of Wyatt, Virgil, and Morgan Earp and J. H. (Doc) Holliday, were placed in the hands of the sheriff, but as Morgan and Virgil Earp were confined to their beds, through wounds received in the late street fight, the warrants were not, in their cases, served, and only Wyatt Earp and Holliday placed under arrest. When those parties were taken before Justice Spicer he denied bail as a matter of right, but upon showing of facts by affidavits, bail was granted and fixed in the sum of $10,000.00 each, being justified in the sum of $20,000.00 for each of the defendants."

November 26, 1881

Excerpt from the testimony of dressmaker, Ms. Addie Bourland, proprietress of the milliner's shop, across the street from the shoot-out scene. Witness for the Defense.

"I am a dressmaker; live opposite the entrance to Fly's lodging house. I first saw five men opposite my house leaning against the small house, west of Fly's. They were Cowboys. One man, (Frank McLaury), was holding a horse, the man with the horse standing outside. Four men, (Earp party), came down the street toward them, and a man with a long coat, (Doc Holliday), walked up to the man holding the horse and put a pistol to his stomach, then stepped back two or three feet, and then the firing became general....I don't know which party fired first, did not see any of the Cowboys throw up their hands....I got up and went into the back room."

"The first thing the Cowboys did when the other party approached them was to raise up and come out to meet them from the side of the house."

November 16, 1881

Excerpt from testimony from Mr. Wyatt B. S. Earp, Defendant.

"....We came upon them close, Frank McLaury, Tom McLaury, and Billy Clanton, standing all in a row against the east side of the building on the opposite side of the vacant place west of Fly's photograph gallery. Ike Clanton and a man I did not know was standing in the vacant space, about half way between the photograph gallery and the next building west. I saw that Billy Clanton, Frank and Tom McLaury had their hands by their sides; Frank McLaury's and Billy Clanton's six-shooters were in plain sight. Virgil said, 'throw up your hands....I have come to disarm you'."

"Billy Clanton and Frank McLaury commenced to draw their pistols; at the same time, Tom

McLaury threw his hand to his right hip, throwing his coat open like that (showing), and jumped behind a horse."

November 22, 1881

Excerpt from the testimony of Mr. Virgil Earp, City Marshal of Tombstone, Defendant.

"….I changed my cane to my left hand, drew my six-shooter and went to fighting.…"

"He, (Tom McLaury), threw his hand back, and followed the movement of the horse around, keeping him as a kind of breastwork. He fired once, if not twice, over the horse's back."

"I fired four shots - one at Frank McLaury and I believe the other three were at Billy Clanton. I am pretty positive one was at Frank McLaury and three at Billy Clanton."

October 27, 1881

Excerpt from feature news article in <u>Tombstone Epitaph</u> newspaper, written by Editor, John P. Clum.

"Mr. Earp, (Virgil), says it was the first shot from Frank McLaury that hit him."

November 26, 1881

Excerpt from the testimony of Mr. Albert C. Bilicke, Proprietor of the Cosmopolitan Hotel in Tombstone. Witness for the Defense.

"….I knew Thomas McLaury by sight in his lifetime. I saw him walking down the south side of Allen Street and enter Everhardy's Butcher Shop; shortly afterwards he came out again, and walked down the street a few steps further, and crossed Allen Street obliquely to the corner of Fourth and Allen Streets, and walked down Fourth Street. This was probably 2 o'clock. When he went into the butcher shop his right-hand pants pocket was flat and appeared as if nothing was in it. When he came out his pants pocket protruded as if there was a revolver therein."

November 26, 1881

Excerpt from the testimony of Mr. J. B. W. Gardiner, Army Surgeon. Witness for the Defense.

"I saw Tom McLaury enter Everhardy's Butcher Shop and quickly re-emerge. I saw no pistol, but supposed, at the time, on seeing the right hand pocket of his pants extending outwards, that he had gotten a pistol."

November 18, 1881

Excerpt from the testimony of Robert S. Hatch, Witness for the Defense.

"….I immediately ran up the street and went into Bauer's butcher shop - the market - probably went as far as the butcher block, near the back end of the shop, turned and went back to the door on the west side of the building; saw Doc Holliday and a man that had been pointed out to me as Frank McLaury, near the middle of Fremont Street, ten or eleven feet apart, or somewhere like that; Frank McLaury made some remark like this: 'I have got you this time'; Holliday made some remark: 'You are a good one if you have', or words to that effect; McLaury seemed to be retreating across the street, to the opposite side of the street; when he got near the adobe building on the opposite side of the street, he stopped and stood with his pistol across his arm, the pistol in his right hand and resting on his left arm, and in the act of shooting; about that time I saw Doc Holliday and Morgan Earp shooting in the direction of McLaury, or at him; Frank McLaury fell to the ground at that time, as if he had been shot; the shooting seemed to be over at that time; I immediately went out of the butcher shop towards Fly's building; before I saw Frank McLaury fall, and before he got across the street, I saw Morgan Earp fall in the middle of the street and I think he made some remark, such as, 'I am hit', or shot, or something of the kind; he, Morgan Earp, immediately got up and commenced to shoot, or was in the act of shooting towards Frank McLaury."

"I saw this man, Fly, come out of his, Fly's, house, with a Henry rifle in his hand. He made the remark, pointing to Billy Clanton below, who had a pistol in his right hand, 'somebody take that pistol away from that man', referring to Billy Clanton. Billy Clanton seemed to be in the act of trying to cock it, but did not seem to have the strength to do so. I said to Mr. Fly, 'go take it yourself, if you want to'. Fly walked towards Billy Clanton and I was right with him. Fly reached down and took hold of the pistol and pulled it out of his hand. As he did so, Billy Clanton said, 'give me some more cartridges'."

October 28, 1881

Excerpt from the testimony of Mr. C. H. Light, resident of Aztec Rooming House, northwest corner of Fremont and Third Streets. Witness for the Coroner's Inquest.

"....saw several men in the act of shooting....Tom McLaury reel and fall on the corner of Fremont and Third....observed three men (of the Earp party) standing at an angle about ten or fifteen feet apart, about the center of the street, facing Fly's photograph gallery....saw another man - Billy Clanton - leaning against the corner of the Harwood House, and a man with a horse - Frank McLaury."

October 29, 1881

Excerpt from the testimony of Mr. B. H. Fallehy. Witness before the Coroner's Inquest.

"....when I got to the corner of Fremont and Fourth, I started to go across to the southwest corner of Fremont; when I got midway between, in the street, I saw the firing had commenced; I kept my eyes on the Earps and Holliday until the shooting commenced; I saw Doc Holliday in the middle of the street; the youngest of the Earp brothers, (Morgan), was about three feet from the sidewalk; he was firing at a man, (Frank McLaury), behind a horse; Holliday also fired at the man behind the horse, and firing at a man, (Tom McLaury), who ran by him on the opposite side of the street; then I saw the man, (Frank McLaury), who had the horse let go, and was staggering all the time until he fell; he had his pistol still when he fell; I never saw the two elder Earps; I did not know where they were situated; I then went to the young man lying on the sidewalk and offered to pick him up; he never spoke except the movement of his lips; I picked up a revolver lying five feet from him; then I saw Doc Holliday running towards where the man was lying, still having a revolver in his hand, making the remark, 'the son-of-a-bitch has shot me and I mean to kill him'; could not say who fired the first shots."

November 26, 1881

Excerpt from the Testimony of (Judge) J. H. Lucas, Probate Court of Tombstone. Witness for the Defense.

"I was in my office on the opposite side of the street....I was sitting in my office. I heard a couple of shots. I then started to the upper hall door. While going, I heard four or five more reports. When I got to the hall door, I cast my eyes up and down the street and saw a man I suppose to have been Billy Clanton in front of the little house just below Fly's building. He had his pistol up and I thought was firing, and for fear of a stray bullet I drew my head in for an instant. I looked again and still saw him standing there with his pistol and I thought fighting. I drew my head in again. I looked again and still saw him with his pistol. I continued to look at him for a moment, and cast my eyes around to see if I could see anyone else that I thought had weapons. I did not see anyone else that I thought had weapons. I think his pistol was discharged twice from the time I thought he was hit till he was down on the ground. I heard some considerable shooting, but could not see any of the parties except Billy Clanton. I am satisfied the shooting came from other parties beside Billy Clanton, though I could not see them."

"....His, (Billy Clanton's), body seemed to bend a little and his pistol was above his head as he seemed to be in the act of falling. I think he caught his hand against the window or wall and turned partly around. He continued to struggle until he got clear down on the ground. About the time he got to the ground, the firing ceased...."

November 23, 1881

Testimony of Mr. R. J. Campbell, Clerk of County Board of Supervisors.
Witness for the Defense.

"The reputation of Frank McLaury was a brave and courageous man and that he was expert in the use of firearms. Ike Clanton is the same. William Clanton, I can't say for him, only by reputation, that he was an expert in the use of firearms. I did not know Tom McLaury only by sight."

November 2, 1881

Excerpt from the testimony of Sheriff John H. Behan. Witness for the Prosecution.

" I saw Frank McLaury on the sidewalk a few feet from the line of the front of the lot."

"The first two shots were fired by the Earp party."

"The nickel-plated pistol was the first fired, and almost instantaneously came two shots right together."

"I looked and saw him, (Frank McLaury), running and a shot was fired and he fell over on his head."

"I heard Morg Earp say, 'I got him'."

November 10, 1881

Excerpt from testimony of Ike Clanton, Witness for the Prosecution.

Question:

"At the time the Earp party came up to where you and the McLaurys and Billy Clanton were standing, what, if anything, did Wyatt Earp do?"

Answer:

"He shoved his pistol against my belly, and said, 'you son-of-a-bitch, you can have a fight'. I turned on my heel and took Wyatt Earp ahold of his hand and pistol with my left hand and grabbed him around the shoulder with my right hand and held him for a few seconds; while I was holding him, he shot and I pushed him around the photograph gallery and jumped into the photograph gallery door; went right through the hall and out the back way, and went off across Allen Street and into the dance hall; as I was leaving, and as I jumped into the door of the photograph gallery, I heard one or two bullets pass right by my head; as I passed through an opening on my way from the gallery, I heard another bullet pass me...."

"There were two horses on the grounds while the shooting occurred. Frank McLaury was holding a horse; Billy Clanton had a horse. There was a Winchester on each horse....Morgan Earp shot William Clanton. I don't know which of the McLaury boys Holliday shot at, but at one of them....I saw his (Morgan's) pistol pointed within two or three feet of his (Billy Clanton's) bosom and saw Billy stagger and fall against the house...."

"....About one o'clock that noon, (before the fight), I was walking up Fourth Street between Allen and Fremont. Virgil Earp came up behind me...Virg Earp struck me on the side of the head, behind the right ear with a six-shooter....Virg Earp took my six-shooter and Winchester away from me...."

October 28-29, 1881

Eyewitness report overheard during the Coroner's Inquest of Mr. R. F. Coleman, concerning the exact moment that he reportedly saw Ike Clanton running into the front door of Fly's Boarding House.

"....one shot fired at him (Clanton), came pretty near to me, and struck a wagon standing in front of Bauer's shop. There was a second shot fired in that direction."

November 8, 1881

Excerpt from the testimony of Mr. William 'Billy' Claibourne, smelting mills worker and wagon driver. Witness for the Prosecution.

"....When they, (Earp party), got to the corner of Fly's building they had their six-shooters in their hands....Frank McLaury had hold of a horse about the corner of the post....Doc Holliday, after the first shots were fired, was shooting at Frank McLaury on the street....There was a Winchester rifle on Frank McLaury's horse, fixed down in the scabbard. During the shooting the horse was in the middle of the street. Frank McLaury had hold of the bridle rein during the shooting....One bullet struck me on the knee of my pants....Doc Holliday shot first, Morgan second, almost together."

November 7, 1881

Excerpts from testimony of Mr. Wesley 'Wes' Fuller. Witness for the Prosecution.

"The first man I was satisfied was hit was Frank McLaury. I saw him staggering and bewildered and I knew he was hit."

"....the Earp party fired the first shots; two shots; almost together."

"....I think Morgan Earp and Doc Holliday fired first; two shots; could not tell."

"....after these shots the firing commenced very rapidly."

"....When firing commenced Frank McLaury was standing by and holding his horse."

"....Billy Clanton was shot through the right wrist. At the time I first saw Frank McLaury draw his pistol, his appearance and action indicated he was shot."

"....I did not see Tom McLaury at the time; I did not see Ike Clanton at the time of the first shooting; I did not see Frank McLaury."

"....there were five or six shots fired by the Earp party before Billy Clanton or Frank McLaury fired and they, Billy and Frank, were the only ones of the Clanton party that I saw fire a shot at all."

"....Frank McLaury drew a weapon and fired some shots during the fight; Frank was in Fremont Street when he drew his weapon; I think he was a little past the middle of the street when he pulled his pistol."

November 10, 1881

Excerpt from the testimony of Mr. J. H. Batcher, Bookkeeper. Witness for the Prosecution.

"....saw Wyatt Earp strike Tom McLaury with his pistol, (before the fight); heard Tom McLaury speak rather loud and said he had always been a friend of his (Earp's); that he had never done a thing against him; Tom McLaury addressed him and after saying something said, 'If you want to fight I am with you'; then Wyatt Earp pulled his gun and asked him (McLaury) if he was heeled. Tom said something, I don't know what; then Wyatt struck him, first with the palm of his hand and then hit him with his right hand with his pistol on the side of his head to once; Tom McLaury fell down and Wyatt Earp walked away, and Tom McLaury got up and left...."

November 4, 1881

Excerpt from testimony of Mrs. M. 'Martha' King, citizen of Tombstone. Witness for the Prosecution.

"I was in the butcher shop on Fremont Street when the shooting occurred; I heard the firing; saw Mr. Holliday with arms; he had a gun; I mean a gun as distinguished from a pistol; he had on an overcoat; the gun on his left hand side, with his overcoat over the gun and his arm thrown over it; I knew it was a gun because his overcoat flew back and I saw it; there were three persons (Earps) with him; I suppose they were; all four were right together, walking in the same direction."

Copyright, 1976

Excerpt from the book, I MARRIED WYATT EARP, The Recollections of Josephine Sarah Marcus Earp, collected and edited by author Glenn G. Boyer, Chapter Five 'Stormy Times', pages 89; 90; 92.

"....Virge still held the cane in his shooting hand, an obvious indication he was really expecting no serious resistance. Frank and Billy placed their hands on their holstered six-shooters. I think this may have been a bluff, even then. Without their trigger-happy friends to help them, this crowd may have hoped to get off and save face with a public mouth battle. Even in the so-called Wild West, shooting members of the police force was not lightly accepted. It could lead to a necktie party in a town like Tombstone, which had a vigilante organization, even though it was a pretty tame excuse for one."

"....Johnny Behan and the adherents of those killed have testified that Doc fired first and Morgan second. This, of course, is absolutely true...."

"After Doc shot Frank McLaury in the belly, Billy Clanton jerked his pistol and aimed at Virge just as Morg shot him in the chest....Billy's shot went wild."

"....even though I was in a panic, I remember the distinct lull that occurred during the shooting. The fight might have ended with the first exchange. Ike Clanton ran. Tom McLaury had ducked behind a horse and hadn't fired yet. But, unfortunately, either Ike, Johnny (Behan), or Ike's friend, Will Allen, fired a sneak shot from the passageway between Fly's house and photo studio. All of the Earps turned in that direction, and at this time, Tom sneaked a shot at Morg, who was closest to him. It hit Morg in the back. Tom had fired it by aiming across the saddle of the horse he was hiding behind. That shot was his sad mistake. Doc had backed a short way into the street out of the smoke. He had reholstered his pistol and held the shotgun ready. Tom got both barrels at short range right after he had fired and turned to run."

"Billy and Frank, both mortally wounded, still showed grit, but couldn't shoot straight anymore. One of them fired a shot that went through the calf of Virgil's leg. After that Virge finished off Billy. Morg, who had been knocked down but risen right up to continue the fight, or perhaps Wyatt or Doc, put the finishing shot into Frank, who was still on his feet, faced off in the road with Doc. Frank's last shot hit Doc in the left hip, but his pistol holster deflected it; he got only a bruise. Morg thought his shot finished Frank. Doc thought his did. Wyatt fired also, but was non-committal on the subject."

"....Wyatt had fired his first shot, contrary to his later testimony, to suppress the fire of the hidden ambusher who tried to get them in the back from Fly's place. Then he snapped a shot at Tom just before Doc got him, but missed Tom and probably grazed the horse, which leaped away, exposing Tom to Doc's fire...."

December 30, 1881

Excerpt of news article featured originally in <u>Kansas City Star</u> newspaper. This interview with eyewitness, Mrs.J. C. Colyer, was re-printed on December 30th in the <u>Tombstone Epitaph</u> newspaper.

"....the Cowboys opened fire on them, (Earps-Holliday), and you never saw such shooting. One of the Cowboys, after he had been shot three times, raised himself on his elbow and shot one of the Officers and fell back dead. Another used his horse as a barricade and shot under its neck...."

December 1, 1881

Excerpt from news article in <u>The Daily Nugget</u> newspaper, Tombstone, Arizona. Opinion of Justice of the Peace Wells Spicer.

"Defendants Wyatt Earp and John H. Holliday, two of the defendants named in the above entitled action, were arrested upon a warrant issued by me on the 29th day of October on a charge of murder. The complaint filed upon which the warrant was issued, accuses said defendants of the murder of William Clanton, Frank McLaury, and Thomas McLaury on the 26th day of last month, at Tombstone, in this county."

"....yet when we consider the condition of affairs incident to a frontier country; the lawlessness and disregard for human life; the existence of a law-defying element in our midst; the fear and feeling of insecurity that has existed; the supposed prevalence of bad, desperate and reckless men who have been a terror to the country, and kept away capital and enterprise, and considering the many threats that have been made against the Earps, I can attach no criminality to his (Marshal Virgil Earp) unwise act. In fact, as the result plainly proves, he needed the assistance and support of staunch and true friends, upon whose courage, coolness and fidelity he could depend in case of an emergency...."

"....I conclude the performance of the duty imposed upon me by saying in the language of the statute: 'There being no sufficient cause to believe the within named Wyatt S. Earp and John H. Holliday guilty of the offense mentioned within, I order them to be released'."

November 1, 1881

Excerpt from The Daily Nugget newspaper, Tombstone, Arizona. Report of the Coroner, H. M. Mathews....

"....Know the cause of the death of William Clanton from that examination of the bodies at the death-house, 9 or 10 o'clock at night, after looking them over casually right after fight; they died from the effects of pistol and gun-shot wounds;....did not examine them thoroughly; there was one two inches from the left nipple, penetrating the lungs; the other was beneath the twelfth rib, above and beneath; 6 inches to the right of the navel; think neither of the wounds went through the body; not probing the wounds cannot say positively what direction they took; both went in front through the body; my opinion was that those wounds were the cause of death; examined the body of Frank McLaury at the same time and day; found in the body of Frank McLaury one wound penetrating the cranium, beneath the right ear; another penetrating the abdomen one inch to the left of the navel. I should say the wound beneath the ear caused instant death - same as if shot through the heart - the wound through the head was at the base of the brain, just beneath the ear;....did not probe that wound; probed it a little; it passed horizontally through the brain; the wound in the abdomen was a straight, penetrating shot; I examined the body of Tom McLaury at the same time and place; found on his body twelve buckshot wounds - on the right side of the body, near together, under the arms, between the third and fifth ribs; my opinion was they were buckshot wounds; laid the palm of my hand over them, it would cover the whole of them, about four inches in space; the wound penetrated straight into the body."

October 27, 1881

Excerpt from feature news article in Tombstone Epitaph newspaper, written by Editor, John P. Clum.

"....The Marshal (Virgil Earp) was shot through the calf of the right leg, the ball going clear through. His brother, Morgan, was shot through the shoulders, the ball entering the point of his right shoulder blade, following across the back, shattering off a piece of one vertebrae and passing out the left shoulder in about the same position that it entered the right....Doc Holliday was hit upon the scabbard of his pistol, the leather breaking the force of the ball so that no material damage was done other than to make him limp a little in his walk...."

Plates Fourteen & Fifteen

The rip-roarious frenetic street fire of DOC HOLLIDAY AND MORGAN EARP dominates this action sequence by Master Artist and Illustrator, Bruce R. Greene, depicting the escape of Cowboy leader, IKE CLANTON, through the front entrance of Fly's Rooming House.

Having jousted briefly with WYATT EARP next to the west wall of Fly's, after the first four shots were fired in the legendary Tombstone confrontation, Ike managed to push Wyatt up against the building, and to bolt straight for the front door. (Extreme left in picture.) In so doing, the blustering, liquored-up outlaw chief brushed right behind VIRGIL EARP, almost causing the City Marshal to lose his balance. In this Illustration, both Virgil, (holding cane), and his more celebrated brother, Wyatt, (to Virgil's left), are trying to quickly compose themselves, mindful of the horrendous blood-letting being unleashed

around them, as the precious seconds tick on.

On Fremont Street, it is out of control. The Earp quartet's two homicidal triggermen, Doc Holliday and Morgan Earp are determined to finish the lethal business they started just moments earlier, when Doc opened fire at FRANK McLAURY, (extreme right holding bridle reins of his horse), and Morgan 'blistered' BILLY CLANTON, (further right of Frank against Harwood House wall, outside of picture), with back-to-back shots to the chest and right hand, respectively. But, despite their crippling wounds, Frank and Billy are not out of it by any means. Doc and Morg both know it. Immediately, the two Earp hell-raisers took aim at McLaury to put the fast-shooting Cowboy out of action, permanently. However, Frank displays an uncanny ability and persistence. Stomach wound, and all, he is able to hang onto his horse with his left hand, while he starts to draw his pistol with his right. In the process, the deadliest of the Cowboy gunmen keeps the bucking horse between himself and the two Earp hit men, denying them a clear shot. (Already Doc and Morgan have fired once each at McLaury, and missed.)

But, even as Doc Holliday was shooting Frank McLaury in the abdomen at the start of the hostilities, he, (Doc), was keenly aware of the wrestling match that was developing between Ike Clanton and Wyatt Earp alongside the Fly's house. (Legend makers will cite Holliday's admonishment of friend and hero, Wyatt Earp, for not gunning down Ike on the spot, when Earp first walked up to the loud-mouthed Cowboy spokesman, face-to-face, in the vacant lot.) Now the venomous Holliday spotted his detestable nemesis, Ike Clanton, making his break out of the killing zone to freedom. Instantly, Doc whirled to his right with such speed and impetuous resolve, that would inspire Wyatt Earp to describe him in later years as, "the quickest man" with a pistol he ever saw. In making such a lightning fast half-twirl in the middle of the street, Holliday is seen here snapping the first of the two strafing shots at Ike Clanton. At the same time, Doc's line of fire 'criss-crosses' with that of his taller comrade in arms, Morgan Earp, the latter seen shooting, (and missing), in the opposite direction at Frank McLaury. Holliday's two near-misses will scare the daylights out of the lily-livered Clanton, both projectiles carooming off the Fly's edifice in an easterly direction. (Left outside of picture). The author believes that Tombstone eyewitness, R. F. Coleman, alluded to these two errant shots by Doc Holliday when Coleman later testified, "One shot fired at him, (Clanton), came pretty near to me, and struck a wagon standing in front of Bauer's shop. There was a second shot fired in that direction". Here is how Ike himself described his close call, "...as I was leaving and as I jumped into the door of the photograph gallery, (Boarding House), I heard one or two bullets pass right by my head"....

Second, after priceless second, the action would accelerate to a rampageous mindless tumult that would become a real fight to the death. The shootists would 'throw lead' in all directions. Anything that moved was fair game. No time to think. It was kill or be killed. In such a wild spectacular melee, gut instinct would take precedent over the more subtle attributes.

And not without further cost to both sides. For each microcasm of time would avail a fresh opportunity, a perilous threat. As Doc Holliday and Morgan Earp are otherwise-occupied in the street, a new menace looms just behind them in the vacant lot along side the other horse, in the form of TOM McLAURY. The 28-year old Tom is also using a horse as a moving rampart to keep it between himself and the shattering Earp cannonade. Tom has now produced a pistol from his right trousers pocket. He intends to bring the weapon into action once he can gain control over the fear-stricken animal next to him. As horse and handler make their way out of the fifteen-foot wide enclosure to the edge of the Harwood House boardwalk, the younger McLaury will get his chance. Helped on further for a second or two, by a 'distraction' that is about to occur in the rear between the Fly's buildings that will seize the attention of all of the Earp group, (including Morgan and Doc), Tom will attack with pernicious effect by shooting over the saddle of the horse, once he pulls abreast of the unsuspecting Morgan Earp at the corner of the post.

However, the sawed-off shotgun seen here obtruding from beneath the left side of Doc Holliday's long gray coat will write a final postscript to Tom McLaury's brief courageous defense that afternoon. Doc, the former dentist turned duelist, will whip out the double-barreled 'instrument of death' in a few moments and turn it with extreme prejudice against the oncoming McLaury. The force of the blast, at such close range, will propel Tom toward the Third Street intersection, (right, outside of the picture), where the hapless Cowboy will collapse, his right rib cage torn by shrapnel. Tom would have only minutes to live.

At this point, it is worth repeating part of the eyewitness testimony of Tombstone laundryman, B. H. Fallehy, who was in the process of crossing Fourth Street at its junction with Fremont, just as the shooting started. This author concludes that Mr. Fallehy must have watched the gun-play on the road from behind the southeast end of The Capital Saloon, where he could peer around the corner, westward, straight down Fremont Street to the next crossroad at Third, and beyond. However, the activity inside of the vacant lot would be 'shut out' from his line of sight, which explains why Mr. Fallehy would state, "....I never saw the two elder Earps; I did not know where they were situated...." Understandable. Both Virgil and Wyatt were positioned beyond the west edge of Fly's Rooming House, inside the lot itself.

The shocking nature of the spectacle then unfolding in the street, as the shooting intensified, must have been terrifying to bystanders running for cover behind the nearest wall, or post, or through the first open door they could find, to dodge the bullets then ricocheting all around them. The fiery duo, Doc Holliday and Morgan Earp, were turning up the heat, and onlooker Fallehy watched it happen. He reported, "I saw Doc Holliday in the middle of the street; the youngest of the Earp brothers, (Morgan), was about three feet from the sidewalk; he was firing at a man, behind a horse; Holliday also fired at the man behind the horse, and firing at a man who ran by him on the opposite side of the street;...."

Author's Supplemental Note:

Frontier scholars who are quick to affix a plot of pre-meditated murder to both Doc Holliday and Morgan Earp on that most storied afternoon in Tombstone, seem to have difficulty reconciling their suspicions, with what appears to be a paradoxical behavior on the part of the two Earp hotheads. On the one hand, Doc and Morg were determined to kill Frank McLaury. On the other hand, they spared his horse. This author has no hesitancy to adhere the belief that Holliday would have shot McLaury's horse, dead, with out batting an eye, and, without even a sense of revulsion or personal regret, if Doc felt that such action was necessary to get at his adversary in the end. As it developed Holliday had time to fire only once, at Frank, during this particular phase of the street battle, because Doc turned his attention to something more compelling, namely, to prevent Ike Clanton from escaping the scene alive.

There is evidence to suggest that Wyatt Earp, the cold-blooded tactician, the player of the odds, would have also killed the horse if presented with a similar circumstance. This author is reminded of Wyatt's instant retaliatory fire against Tom McLaury, (a few seconds further into the fight), when Earp observed Tom shooting at pet-brother, Morgan, from over the saddle of Billy Clanton's horse. Wyatt's first bullet inflicted a painful charring wound on the animal causing it to spook, and to race away from its helmsman. But Earp seems to have been prepared to destroy the horse to get at his brother's assailant in the final outset. (Doc got there first and with decisive effect.)

As noted previously, Morgan Earp did shoot twice at the elder McLaury, (Frank), in the street, at close range and in the opening seconds of the conflict. The Cowboy's deft usage of his horse as a protective shield, is attributable to Morgan's ineffective shot making at that moment. (The youngest of 'The Fighting Earps', that day, would not miss on his third, and last attempt, when the animal tore away from Frank finally giving Morgan a clear field of fire, as the showdown neared its finale in the remaining five seconds.) That Morg should present Earpiana researchers with such a duality of purpose remains part of the continuing controversy as to the 'real essence' of the Earp brothers. For the 30-year old Morgan, while regarded by most historians as the carousing buddy of the notorious Doc Holliday, and equally as unpredictable and minacious, is also seen as personally inviting and jovial; a sort of 'devil-may-care', in the context of being a good sport, and an affectionate, protective family man. Mrs. Virgil 'Allie' Earp speaks of Morg in this kind of endearing manner in Frank Waters', albeit rampantly negative, book, The Earp Brothers of Tombstone. In Glenn G. Boyer's more straightforward and objective volume, I Married Wyatt Earp, 'Josie' Earp expresses a similar pro-Morgan sentiment. Ditto, Wells Fargo undercover agent, Fred J. Dodge, in Carolyn Lake's 1969 work about the stage line detective's career exploits. Hence, it would not be surprising that Morgan Earp had taken care not to have harmed Frank McLaury's horse, yet all the while, tried to snuff out its owner.

Perhaps we should ponder the relevance of a brief vocal exchange between Morg and his older brother, the 'Iceman' himself, Wyatt Earp, as the four law enforcers started on their 'walk with destiny' down Fourth Street to eventually confront the Clanton-McLaury Cowboys in the vacant lot. Wyatt would testify later, "Morgan Earp said to me, 'They (Cowboys) have horses; had we not better get some horses ourselves, so that if they make a running fight we can catch them? "I said, 'No, if they try to make a running fight we can kill their horses, and then capture them'."

Kill their horses, and then capture them. Not kill the Cowboys, said Wyatt....'capture them'.

In contrast, Morg might have thought to, 'kill the Cowboys, but save the horses'.

Virgil? Don't kill anyone, or anything. Instead, 'arrest them'.

As for Doc Holliday, what would it matter? To kill man, or beast, would probably have been of no consequence to the one member of the Earp party who, it seems for certain, just wanted to get on with it.

So goes the never-ending story about the Earp Brothers and Doc Holliday, and about their true state of minds on that immortal day in the history of the Old West.

Little wonder. After 110 years, the debate continues....

"DESPERATE MEN AND A DESPERATE ENCOUNTER"

"....A bad time yesterday when Wyatt, Virgil, and Morgan Earp with Doc Holliday had a street fight with the two McLaurys and Bill Clanton and Ike, all but the latter being killed and V. and M. Earp wounded. Desperate men and a desperate encounter. Bad blood brewing for some time and I am not surprised at the outbreak. It is only a wonder it has not happened before...."

George W. Parsons, Citizen of Tombstone,
as he recorded in his personal diary.
October 27, 1881.

Part Two

Author's Working Notes

VISIT TO TOMBSTONE:

This author, having read a good many accounts during the past thirty years by well-known authorities of the Earp-Clanton gun battle on Fremont Street, and of the Tombstone era in general, was privileged to visit that most mythological of Frontier towns during mid-March of this year (1991). To say that I was deeply moved and inspired by the experience would be an understatement. Remarkably, some of the key buildings and localities directly relevant to the subject matter herein, have been preserved down through the past 110 years. Other facilities have been reconstructed to a state of original appearance. Some important, strategic landmarks have been designated as National Historic Sites, thereby ensuring perpetuity for this most precious of old western treasures.

Not surprisingly, sentiment on the part of citizens who live and work within the Tombstone environs, continues to be divided to this day, as to the 'true' characters of the Earp brothers, namely, Virgil, Wyatt, and Morgan, and of their controversial ally, Doc Holliday. Too, the morality of the 'Gunfight at the O.K. Corral' persists as the centerpiece of spirited debate as to whether the gun-play was justified; whether the Earps and Holliday were actually guilty of homicidal murder; whether the showdown could have been avoided by dutiful professional restraint on the part of the Officers; or, conversely, whether it was the Cowboys who were the real instigators of the affray, that, after a series of threats, provocations, and near incidents leading up to the gunfire on the afternoon of October 26, 1881, the Earp brothers and Doc Holliday were left with little choice but to shoot-to-kill.

Such an argument will ensue far beyond the lifetime of this author, and of the reader of this work. As rightfully it should. For such is the nature of this most tantalizing subject of our American frontier past.

But, this author wishes to put his cards on the table, at this outset, by withdrawing from any discussion, pro or con, as to which of the group of combatants were 'in the right', so to speak. For there are writers and researchers far better versed, and in possession of much formidable documentation that qualifies them to speak with more validity on the subject. With recognition of the vast amount of investigative material that has been accrued and subsequently pledged to the Tombstone saga during the past century, this author is first to salute all of those writers and historians who have dedicated their efforts to such end. Thank God for them. For without their magnificent enterprise, such armchair enthusiasts like me would never be exposed to the opportunity....to the privilege....of throwing our hats in the ring, to join such a lively forum.

This author therefore leaves the ethics of the O.K. Corral episode to those who are better able and equipped to deal with it. My interest centers on the actual shoot-out and with a version of the event that came to me gradually, as I walked the streets of Tombstone. I strolled through the O.K. Corral. I studied the buildings. I talked to some of the townsfolk. I wandered through the Boot Hill Cemetery. Most significantly, I purchased two books while touring the city that I had not had the opportunity to read before.

The first, <u>The Chronicles of Tombstone</u>, was by Tombstone resident and well-known Earp writer, Ben T. Traywick. The second was by the reputable Earp authority, Glenn G. Boyer, and was his biographical depiction of the life of Wyatt Earp's third wife, Mrs. Josephine 'Josie' Sarah Marcus Earp, in the form of her memoirs, aptly titled, <u>I Married Wyatt Earp</u>.

As I read these two fantastic publications, far into the night, in my hotel room across from the Boot Hill burial ground, I became enamored of a version of the gunfight, and of a sequence of events that began to finally put the pieces into my own puzzle of the past thirty years. I began to envision what might have actually occurred; when; and between whom; during the so-called thirty seconds that the shooting was thought to have entailed by eyewitnesses.

"It lasted thirty seconds, with about thirty shots fired", said one old-timer to me, in a bar in Tombstone on the afternoon I arrived to see the place for myself.

Thirty seconds. Just like that. A nonchalant, almost flippant reference in a conversation over a few beers. Thirty seconds. Tomorrow, the conversation would be forgotten to the old-timer. So, too, would the tourist sitting in front of him asking all of those 'damned fool' questions about what happened 110 years ago. How many people must visit with the old-timer each year, full of such inquiries, and anxious to compare notes and expertise.

How many visitors come to ask about....'the most famous thirty seconds in the history of the Old West'.

This writer now subscribes to the following assumptions, and to the events thereto, that comprise the shoot-out scenario from start to finish....those infamous thirty seconds:

WHERE THEY STOOD:

That, contrary to the mass of opinion that the Earps and Doc Holliday entered the vacant lot, just west of Fly's Rooming House, with Virgil to the extreme left and innermost in the lot; Wyatt next, and to his right; with Morgan and Doc Holliday, in that order, spread out into Fremont Street, this author now believes that the actual deployment of the Earp party was constituted by Wyatt, not Virgil, being the farthest in, with Virgil, Morgan, and Doc Holliday to his (Wyatt's) right, and in that order.

That, in furtherance to the above, Ike Clanton was away and east from the wall of the Harwood House, which building marked one extremity of the vacant lot; the two Fly's buildings, (boarding house and photography shack), being the eastern boundary of the showdown site. Ike Clanton would have had to be nearest to the entrance of Fly's if he was to eventually struggle with Wyatt Earp; shake off Wyatt after a few seconds; and take the route of shortest escape from the scene of the chaos, namely, around the Fremont Street corner of Fly's Boarding House, and into its front door. If Ike were to have been standing at the rear of the vacant lot, he would have instinctively headed for the middle alley, between the boarding house and the photo shack. In times of panic, and in the midst of murderous mayhem, one is still inclined to find the nearest exit. The claim that Virgil was first into the vacant lot, with Wyatt to his right, does not reconcile with eyewitness testimony, (including that of Wyatt Earp and Ike Clanton), that upon entering the lot, Wyatt walked up to Ike Clanton; put his pistol to Clanton's stomach; and challenged him. With an already congested enclosure...nine combatants in a space of just fifteen feet, including two horses...how was Virgil Earp expected to address the Cowboy crowd with any degree of authority; hold a cane aloft; and be minded by his antagonists, let alone even be seen, if Ike Clanton was also supposed to be standing there with a revolver in his gut, (as pointed by Wyatt), both of these confronters to Virgil's immediate right? And, in the fierce but brief struggle between Wyatt and Ike during the early sconds of the fracas, how, and what, was Virgil to do, short of hauling off and attacking Clanton himself; which he (Virgil) did not do?

That, this author is satisfied that Billy 'The Kid' Claibourne was not a shooting participant in the thirty second melee. It was Billy who stood deepest in the vacant lot, nearest to the O.K. Corral to the rear (south). The shortest route of escape for the twenty-one year old Claibourne, was therefore, rightward, and straight for the space between the two Fly's buildings. In so making this dash out of the rear of the vacant lot, he, (Claibourne), would have had to come awfully close to the grappling duo of Wyatt Earp and Ike Clanton. Wyatt's pistol being already out of its holster, and with Ike holding Earp's gun arm away from the line of fire, makes it plausible, (to this author), that Wyatt's gun discharged, and that the bullet grazed the trouser leg of Billy Claibourne as he sped by and out of the area.

That, the foregoing errant shot that brushed Billy Claibourne's pants, was therefore one of the first reports to be heard by nearby witnesses when the hostilities commenced. It was one of a grouping of five shots, (in the opinion of this author), that opened the bedlam, just before a 'pause' of a few seconds, which short interlude is almost universally reported by all Tombstoners who 'listened' to the fight.

That, to complete this author's visual picture of the whereabouts, within the vacant lot, of the Cowboy shootists, looking westward, (in the direction of the Harwood House), from left to right: Ike Clanton, nearest to the Fly's building and to its Fremont Street frontage; Billy Claibourne, deepest (south) within the lot; Tom McLaury, with Billy Clanton's horse just behind, and between him and Billy; and finally, to the extreme right, slightly out into Fremont Street and holding a horse, Frank McLaury. In being so situated, Wyatt stood opposite Ike Clanton; Virgil opposite both Tom McLaury and Billy Clanton; Morgan obliquely opposite Billy Clanton and standing beyond the boundary line of the vacant lot toward the end of the boardwalks to the street; and Doc Holliday, beyond the same boardwalks, definitely out on Fremont Street, threatening Frank McLaury.

THE PAUSE:

That, there appeared to nearby listeners to be a slight pause following the opening shots, (herewith attributed to Doc Holliday; Morgan Earp; Billy Clanton; and to the accidental discharge of Wyatt's revolver), seems perfectly understandable. To shoot to kill, under such conditions, one would need to have a target. What targets could be presented, if we are to try to imagine the scene following the first series of shots? The two horses, despite any expert claims that such animals could be controlled in such a cramped and smoke-filled compound, must have been a major problem to their handlers, to say the least. The preponderance of testimony indicates that immediately upon receiving Doc Holliday's first pistol shot to his belly, Frank McLaury, and his bucking horse, started to move out to the middle of Fremont Street to the opposite side, before the frightened animal finally broke free and galloped eastward toward Fourth Street out of the area. Again, eyewitnesses will later report that Frank held onto the horse's reins with his left hand, which hand he also clutched at his bleeding abdomen while he drew his six-shooter with his right. Author Ben Traywick, in his book, cites the reprint, (in the <u>Tombstone Epitath,</u> December 30, 1881 edition), of an interview with a Mrs. J. C. Colyer, that appeared earlier in the <u>Kansas City Star.</u> In this story, Mrs. Colyer, claiming to be an eyewitness to the gunfight from her vantage point on the corner of Fourth and Fremont Streets, looking westward down Fremont, said, "Another (Cowboy) used his horse as a barricade and shot under its neck". This writer accepts this 'Cowboy' to be Frank McLaury, shooting under his horse's neck, with the animal between himself and the Earp party. But, before Frank was to get control of his horse to the point of being able to rein it in, to reach under its neck to fire from the middle of the street, he would first have had to get there. In so doing, this author believes that the horse may have tugged at its reins, (after being spooked by the first gun shots), and actually half-dragged the critically-wounded McLaury out to the center of the street. That means that Morgan Earp and Doc Holliday probably jumped out of the way of the oncoming frenzied animal. The horse, dragging its rider with it, would doubtless head away from the roar of the shots and from the acerbic gunsmoke fumes, and would look for the nearest open space....the other side of the street.

In undertaking this exit from the area, and remembering the survivalist instincts of the ever-dangerous, (albeit mortally wounded), Frank McLaury, it would seem intuitive that Frank would try to keep the horse between himself and his adversaries. Or, are we to only credit his brother Tom with possessing the ability to use a horse as a shield on that day? More on the younger McLaury later. This author's scenario of Frank McLaury being pulled by his horse backing out into the street around, and past, Doc Holliday and Morgan Earp, (themselves dancing out of the way of the spooked animal), would momentarily remove McLaury as a hittable target for Doc and Morg. A pause. No shooting here.

That, meanwhile, in the vacant lot, Wyatt Earp and Ike Clanton were engaged in a wrestling match near the northwest wall of Fly's Boarding House. A pause. No shooting here.

That, Virgil Earp, under this author's interpretation of the tragedy, was standing transfixed in stark disbelief of the horrific events around him; holding his cane in the air; and with 'the pause' then in effect, must have been hoping for dear life that the shooting would stop, then and there. No shooting from Virgil. Not at this time, anyway....

That, Billy Claibourne was long gone, having bolted into Fly's Boarding House and away from the pandemonium. No shooting here.

That, Tom McLaury, according to this author's depiction of the opening events, grabbed the reins of Billy Clanton's horse; jumped behind it; was reaching for a pistol in his right pants pocket; and was trying to control the animal by holding the saddle horn at the same time. This fifteen foot-wide vacant lot could only afford so much room to maneuver. It makes acute sense to this author that the horse, obviously scared out of its wits, was then in the act of looking for the fastest route to follow the other panic-stricken animal out of the area into the street. That means that the horse had to pass in front of Billy Clanton, on its way out of the vacant lot, with Tom McLaury right along with it. For a brief pause, the younger McLaury was no target for any shooter. Wyatt was in a tussle. Virgil was holding a cane. And, Doc and Morg were otherwise occupied out in the street trying to dodge the other McLaury's on-charging animal, not to mention guarding against that stellar pistoleer, Frank McLaury himself. Were Morgan Earp and Doc Holliday to turn their attention to Tom McLaury at that exact moment, what would they have had to shoot at? Nothing. Tom was behind the other horse....

That, so was the wounded Billy Clanton. He had to be protected for a few seconds by the animal as it fought its way into Fremont Street. This author's version of the initial seconds of the gunfight, denotes Billy as absorbing two hits, back-to-back, from Morgan Earp's weapon....one in the left chest....and the other, a crippling shot to Billy's right gun hand. In that the 19-year old Cowboy was practically standing against the wall of the Harwood House when the shooting started, it is logical to assume that the impact of Morgan Earp's first bullet slammed Billy up against the building. While Billy was in the act of switching his pistol from his shattered right hand to his left, (and leaning against the Harwood wall trying to keep on his feet), he was hidden from view by the horse struggling in front of him, with Tom McLaury in control. No targets here. The pause.

THE SHOOTING RESUMED:

That, it is the belief of this author that City Marshal Virgil Earp was not intent on bringing matters to a shooting, if such a calamity could have been avoided on that afternoon of October 26, 1881. From all accounts, Virgil seems to have seriously applied himself to his duties as a Peace Officer in Tombstone throughout his tenure in that city. On occasion he even arrested members of his own family and several other acquaintances of the Earp clan, for minor infractions. The Marshal, although the oldest of 'The Fighting Earps' of Tombstone, appeared to acquiesce to Wyatt in important matters of strategy. This seems to have contributed to the long-standing resentment between Virgil's wife, Allie, and Wyatt, with Mrs. Earp distrusting Wyatt and blaming him for the tragedy that was to befall the Earp clan in Tombstone after the O.K. Corral bloodbath. There is just no argument against the assertion that if Virgil really wanted to murder the Cowboys, he, as an Officer of the Law, could have shot them on sight during the hours prior to the row on Fremont Street. To wit, Virgil had previously disarmed Ike Clanton of a six-shooter and a Winchester on Fourth Street in the face of homicidal threats against the Earps, attributed to Ike by eyewitnesses. Instead of killing Clanton, the Marshal, (accompanied by brother Morgan), pistol-whipped the Cowboy and hauled him off to jail, where Ike was fined twenty-five dollars for illegally carrying weapons. Instead of carrying the sawed-off shotgun himself to the O.K. Corral ruckus, and using it, Virgil, the 'Gentle Ben' of the Earp group, preferred to hold Doc Holliday's cane, and, as witnesses would attest, it was Virgil who made the demand to the Cowboys to surrender their guns and to throw up their hands.

That, in terms of years of experience and heralded accomplishments as an Officer of the Law, this author adheres to the belief that Wyatt Earp, the most renowned of 'The Fighting Earps', was, himself, not prone to violence if such recourse could have been avoided. Again, who can argue against Wyatt's peaceful motives, when he (Earp), instead of shooting Tom McLaury on the street outside of the Courthouse, earlier that day, buffaloed the younger McLaury with his long-barreled pistol, and walked away, leaving Tom sprawled in the street. Shortly after this incident, Wyatt found himself in a face-off against Billy Clanton and Frank McLaury, both packing revolvers on their hips, in front of Spangenburg's Gun Shop on Fourth Street. Here again, a confrontation was avoided when Wyatt prudently backed away from the scene. If anything, the attitude of Wyatt Earp on the afternoon of October 26, 1881, seems ambivalent to the prospect of a killing. The most secretive and most calculating of the Earps; the player of the odds; the leader of the group of brothers; Wyatt said it best, when he testified at his murder trial the following month that he told Ike Clanton that he, (Wyatt), would avoid a fight if he could help it because "there was no money in it".

That, it is to the ill-tempered, fractious Doc Holliday that this author concludes must rest the cause for the tragic shoot-out. While Wyatt and Virgil could avoid an armed clash and club an opponent over the head with their guns, as opposed to blasting him into eternity, not so with the ungovernable Doc Holliday. As would be part of courtroom testimony the following month, Ike Clanton would swear that Doc threatened him and called him out to a duel the night before the Fremont Street gun battle. This unruly encounter, coming on the heels of a long tense period of distrust, accusations, and threats between the Earps and the Cowboys, was now being fueled by the last-minute deputization of Holliday to assist Marshal Virgil Earp to disarm the Cowboy crowd. It was all too much for the rampageous Doc Holliday to resist. The shoot-first-discuss-it-later former dentist, opened fire at point-blank range at Frank McLaury, and thereby started the whole apocalyptic episode in the street. And, after the pause? Forget any lofty illusions that the shooting could have come to an early halt. Not with Mr. Holliday present, thank you. As soon as the gambling gun thrower spotted his detestable enemy, Ike Clanton, escaping from the vacant lot via the front door of the Fly's house, the nickel-plated Colt pistol of Doc Holliday spoke again....and again. So much for lofty illusions.

That, Morgan Earp, handsome, youthful and impetuous, (and prone to idolizing his roustabout buddy, Doc Holliday), was also guilty of the shoot-first modus operandi on that dark day in the turbulent history of the Old West. Morg opened fire with Doc and must also bear the responsibility for the start of enmities. The pause? Dismiss the thought. As soon as Doc cut loose at Ike Clanton, Morgan saw simultaneous opportunity to finish Frank McLaury's business too. He started shooting at the elder McLaury behind the horse. The fight then started to become general.

THE DISTRACTION:

That, with such Clanton-McLaury supporters as Sheriff John H. Behan; Billy 'The Kid' Claibourne; Will 'Billy' Allen; and Wes Fuller; all taking refuge in and near the Fly's Boarding House, next to bullets flying just outside in the vacant lot, this author cannot imagine how it allegedly came to pass that one, or two, of these Cowboy heroes did not take a hand to at least cover Ike's retreat out of the area. That the roisterous Ike should abandon his teenage brother to such blistering fire from the hated Earps is hard enough to swallow. Running through the Fly's building at top speed, slamming doors in the process as he made his exit, would surely cause some commotion. To the Cowboy advocates previously mentioned, add the presence of Camillus S. Fly himself, in his own house, and maybe others. Could these people have just sat there cringed in their boots, in a vow of silence, while outside all around them must have sounded like the end of the world? In her memoirs by Glenn G. Boyer, Mrs. Josephine 'Josie' Earp relates that a distraction of some kind did take place....a pistol shot, or two....from the alleyway between the two Fly's buildings, and that this noise caused the Earp brothers to turn toward the direction of the disturbance. In that Ike Clanton would later testify that a bullet barely missed him as he passed between the two houses, this author attributes such an attempt to the Earp closest to the retreating Ike Clanton....the Earp innermost in the vacant lot....Wyatt. No other of the Marshal's group could have fired such a shot. Doc and Morg were out in the street and too far removed. For them to fire into the lot after Clanton would endanger both Virgil and Wyatt in the line of fire. Virgil? Not yet. This author still places the Marshal, at this stage of the gunfight, as not having drawn his weapon.

Plates Sixteen & Seventeen

"But, unfortunately, either Ike, (Clanton), Johnny, (Behan), or Ike's friend, Will Allen, fired a sneak shot from the passageway between Fly's house and the photo studio. All of the Earps turned in that direction, and at this time, Tom, (McLaury), sneaked a shot at Morg, (Earp), who was closest to him. It hit Morg in the back. Tom had fired it by aiming across the saddle of the horse he was hiding behind."

Mrs. Wyatt 'Josie' Earp from
her recollections in the book
I Married Wyatt Earp
by Glenn G. Boyer

"....saw several men in the act of shooting....Tom McLaury reel and fall on the corner of Fremont and Third....observed three men, (of the Earp party), standing at an angle about ten or fifteen feet apart, about the center of the street, facing Fly's photograph gallery....saw another man - Billy Clanton - leaning against the corner of the Harwood House, and a man with a horse - Frank McLaury."

C. H. Light, Eyewitness and Resident
of Aztec Rooming House on northside
corner of Fremont and Third Streets

Here we seem to have two versions of the same event, 'The Distraction'. The first is told by Wyatt Earp's widow from her conversations with her famous husband over the forty-eight year period following the legendary street fight in 1881, to Wyatt's death on January 13, 1929. The second is from Tombstone eyewitness, C. H. Light, independently reporting what he saw as he watched the shooting from his quarters at the Aztec Rooming House on the northside corner of Fremont and Third Streets, diagonally opposite the scene of the shoot-out.

The obvious contradiction between the two accounts concerns the actions of Tom McLaury and Morgan Earp. But is there really a contradiction? Let us examine the two versions more closely.

Mrs. Josie Earp has Tom McLaury firing at Morgan Earp from over the saddle of the horse as all of the Earps were 'distracted' by a commotion, a gun shot, emanating from the alleyway between the two Fly's houses. It is the contention of this author that Ike Clanton was then in the act of making a head-long dash between the Fly's buildings, to effect his escape out of the back, (south), door of the photo shack to the open lot leading to Allen Street, and beyond, to safety. It is therefore plausible that one of Clanton's cronies, then in refuge in the front Fly's property, could have attempted to shoot at the Earps to lay down a protective fire to mask Ike's retreat. Or, in a moment of emotional outrage, the same attacker could have tried to retaliate at the sight of Billy Clanton and Frank McLaury being overwhelmed by the initial Earp barrage.

At the same time, Wyatt Earp, according to this author, was standing deepest in the vacant lot and nearest to the threat from the passageway between the two buildings. He whirled and fired, once, just missing Ike's head as the Cowboy leader sped between the two structures. In sworn testimony later, Clanton was to state, "....as I passed through an opening on my way from the gallery, I heard another bullet pass me".

Before Wyatt could press his response against the hidden ambusher, an even greater threat was emerging in the form of Tom McLaury's attack of Morgan Earp, toward the street corner of the Harwood House boardwalk. Wyatt immediately turned back to his right and fired at Tom, missing McLaury, but winging the horse, causing it to bolt out of the area. That left Tom open to the shotgun blitz of Doc Holliday further out on Fremont Street.

In examining the positions of the other shootists at this time, the eyewitness account of C. H. Light, compared to the claims of this author, vary little, if at all. For example, Frank McLaury, "with a horse", is depicted by this author as being on the street. (In fact, the so-called 'Distraction' allowed Frank the few precious seconds to put more 'daylight' between himself and the otherwise-occupied Doc Holliday and Morgan Earp by quickly moving with the horse toward the opposite side of the road.) Billy Clanton is standing against the Harwood House, having just taken two bullet wounds as the direct result of Morgan Earp's opening fire. Mr. Light does not mention Ike Clanton. This author has already asserted that Ike was, at that moment, practically out of the immediate area of the vacant lot. Too, Billy Claibourne is not identified. Understandable. The so-called 'Arizona Billy The Kid' was already through the rear door of the main Fly's house, and out of sight. Wyatt Earp would not be easily visible to an eyewitness looking obliquely at the shoot-out scene from the corner of Fremont and Third Streets, because at some point, the viewer's glance into the vacant lot would be blocked by the corner of the Harwood House. But the same onlooker could see the entrance to the lot, and the frontage of the Fly's and Harwood Houses. Hence, when C. H. Light refers to only, "three men, (of the Earp party), standing at an angle about ten or fifteen feet apart, about the center of the street, facing Fly's photography gallery", that could only mean, (to this author), that the fourth Earp, Wyatt, deep inside the vacant lot, was then out of Mr. Light's view. From Mr. Light's position, Doc Holliday, Morgan and Virgil Earp would appear to be standing almost in a row, on the street, with Virgil, (his back to the corner of Fly's Boarding House), being the farthest away of the three from observer Light.

Which only leaves Tom McLaury's location to answer for. Therein lies the big question. When C. H. Light stated that he saw, "Tom McLaury reel and fall on the corner of Fremont and Third", did he mean that Tom went down at the precise same moment that he, (Light), also saw the three Earp members facing toward the Fly's property? A few seconds later, and McLaury would in fact go down, under shotgun blitzkrieg from Doc Holliday, after Tom first wounded Morgan from behind the horse, while he, (Morgan), was momentarily preoccupied with 'The Distraction' from in between the Fly's buildings.

Which causes this author to wonder if eyewitnesses viewing such a multi-person life and death tragedy, in the heat of the moment and ducking the bullets in the process, do not have the tendency to enhance their accounts, afterward, by juxtaposing what they actually saw happen, with what they came to know as also happened, after the fact.

Author's Supplemental Note:

In this picture, Master Artist and Illustrator, Bruce R. Greene, has tried to capture that exact moment when all members of the Earp quartet were believed to be preoccupied with 'The Distraction', in between the two Fly's buildings. Wyatt Earp, now positioned deepest in the vacant lot, has already whirled to his left, and instinctively fired a shot at the source of the disturbance. Wyatt's near miss is theorized by the author to have whizzed by the head of Ike Clanton as the Cowboy leader made his successful break to freedom from the back door of the main Fly's edifice.

Even though Doc Holliday, (with long gray coat on Fremont Street), has also been temporarily diverted by the ruckus at the rear, (south), of the lot, the speed-shooting Doc still has the side-eyed presence of mind to detect the now oncoming threat, in his direction, of Tom McLaury. For Tom has successfully worked aside Billy Clanton's horse to the vantage point shown here, both animal and handler about to emerge from the immediate area of the deathful fifteen foot-wide enclosure. The horse will make it. Tom will not. In firing the first of two back-to-back shots at Morgan Earp, from over the saddle of the horse, (the initial attempt shown here just missing the unsuspecting Morgan standing next to Holliday), McLaury will instantly enrage both Doc and Wyatt Earp. Wyatt will twirl back to his right and quickly loose two bullets at favorite brother Morgan's attacker. Both will miss. But, the first will graze the horse's mane, causing it to tear away from its holder and to speed out of the vacant lot down Fremont Street. But, before losing control of the horse, Tom McLaury will score a hit with his second shot. The slug will rip through Morgan's shoulders, across the back, (right to left), and 'drop' Morg in his tracks, to the road. Meanwhile, the inflamed, vengeful Doc Holliday has begun to switch weapons. He has already started to reholster his nickel-plated Colt six-shooter on his right hip, after having just strafed Ike Clanton with it twice, as the cowardly outlaw chief escaped through the front entrance of the main Fly's house. With his other arm, Doc commences to unfurl the sawed-off shotgun from beneath the left side of his overcoat, fully intending to bring the slaughterous cannon into action against Tom McLaury at the very first opportunity. Doc will get his wish in a second or two. Tom's fear-stricken horse will hurl him straight at Holliday. The stumbling Cowboy is about to meet his maker, up close, almost eyeball to eyeball, and take a fatal load of twelve buckshot charges in his right ribs.

Tom's older brother, Frank, (extreme left), has also taken advantage of the 'distracted' Earp party, by swiftly maneuvering with his own horse toward the opposite side of the street. Critically wounded, Frank has finally jerked his pistol. He will tighten up on the reins of his horse with his left hand and steady the trembling animal. Crouching low, McLaury will reach under the horse's neck with his fully-extended right shooting arm, and will open fire at Tombstone City Marshal, Virgil Earp, barely seen on the other side of Frank's horse, at the corner of Fly's Boarding House, unaware of the older McLaury's threatening presence. The Marshal is about to get caught in a crossfire, of sorts. With Tom McLaury's horse now just about out of the way, 19-year old Billy Clanton, (across from Virgil), will have a clear field of fire to right himself against the wall of the corner of the Harwood House, and to start shooting at Virgil in earnest, even though the gutsy teenager has already been pummeled by Morgan Earp's opening salvo.

That, while on the subject of 'The Distraction', the just-described Ike Clanton run-out may not have been the only such diversion that emanated from the crowded Fly's Rooming House. The eyewitness report of C. H.Light, from his residence at the Aztec Rooming House, on the northwest corner of Fremont and Third Streets, is titillating, to be sure. Mr. Light states...."saw several men in the act of shooting....Tom McLaury reel and fall on the corner of Fremont and Third....observed three men, (of the Earp party), standing at an angle about ten or fifteen feet apart, about the center of the street, facing Fly's photography gallery....saw another man - Billy Clanton - leaning against the corner of the Harwood House, and a man with a horse - Frank McLaury". This scene could be of the Earps confronting YET ANOTHER distraction from the direction of Fly's house, in this case after Tom McLaury had been shot down by Doc Holliday. Or, it could be of that exact moment when both Doc and Morg were turning toward the blistering exchange of gunfire between Virgil Earp and Billy Clanton. In such a sequence, Doc would have just levied both buckshot charges at Tom McLaury; discarded the shotgun; re-drawn his pistol; and now would be in the act of getting back into the action behind, or to his left. Morg, already felled by a shot in the back from the now dying Tom McLaury, would have arisen and would be in the act of rejoining the firestorm. However, and in a second, both Doc and Morg would do an 'about face', of sorts, to meet the threat across the street in the person of Frank McLaury, himself about to lose the protection of his horse, thereby opening the Cowboy to a fight-ending barrage from Holliday, Morgan and Wyatt Earp. This author assumes the third Earp in the C. H. Light account to be Virgil, then in the process of a point-blank six-shooter free-for-all with the gravely-wounded Billy Clanton, the latter now having edged himself to the corner of the Harwood House and on the verge of a downslide to the ground.

That, what of the whereabouts of Wyatt Earp? From the oblique line of sight offered from the northwest corner of Fremont and Third Streets, observer C. H. Light would seem to be the only eyewitness, from this angle, to have been in such close proximity to the shoot-out scene and to have commanded a view of the street; the front of the Fly's building; and the entrance to the vacant lot just west of it. However, while Mr. Light would be able to view the streetside opening to the vacant lot, he would not be able to see all the way into the lot itself, for, at some point, his line of sight would be blocked by the corner of the Harwood House. It is this author's opinion that at the time that Mr. Light was looking at the shoot-out scene, Wyatt Earp had stepped more into the center of the lot so that he could get a clear shot, north-eastward, out of the enclosure at Frank McLaury, who was, at that same time, on the other side of Fremont Street. In a moment, and in the opinion of this author, four gunshots were to be fired almost as one; Frank McLaury at Doc Holliday; Doc back at Frank; Morgan Earp at Frank; and Wyatt, having to shoot over the greatest distance from inside the lot, his bullet passing right between Virgil and Billy Clanton. These four shots, fired at the same moment that Virgil Earp shot Billy Clanton in the pants leg near the right knee, ended the Fremont Street catastrophe.

THE WOUNDING OF MORGAN EARP:

That, after the heretofore-described distraction from the Fly's building, Mrs. Josephine Earp (in the book, I Married Wyatt Earp), goes on to claim that it was Tom McLaury, firing from behind and over the saddle of a horse, that shot Morgan Earp in the shoulder as Morgan's attention was directed toward the commotion within the vacant lot. Is this possible? Would someone, in this modern day, dare to support this claim, in the face of overwhelming opinions to the contrary, that it was actually Billy Clanton who wounded Morg? And what of the testimony by Clanton backers that Tom McLaury was unarmed?

That, this author understands that the bullet entered Morgan's right shoulder, sped across the entire width of the back, even tipping the backbone, and finally exiting out of the left shoulder.

That, this author is hard pressed to accept the supposition that Billy Clanton, already shot in the left lung, his gun hand crippled, and firing with his other hand, all the while trying to keep his balance by leaning against the Harwood House wall, could have been the one to have fired the bullet into Morgan Earp, the latter standing obliquely toward Fremont Street. This would have had to be some shot, a lucky one at that, not to mention the almost super-human effort needed by Billy to accomplish the feat.

That, this author depicts Morgan Earp as in the act of turning from firing at Frank McLaury, on Fremont Street, rightward, to face the vacant lot and the scene of the distraction between the two Fly's buildings. At such an angle presented by Morgan, an adversary, (in order to shoot Morg through the right shoulder), would have to be located more north, as well as westward, like, say, out toward Fremont, almost on line with Third Street.

That, this author is inclined to support the claim of Mrs. Wyatt Earp, and Tombstone author, Mr. Ben T. Traywick, that it was actually Tom McLaury, firing over the saddle of the horse, that put the slug through the right shoulder of Morgan Earp. This shot was made at the time that McLaury had just crossed with the horse in front of Billy Clanton, over the streetside boundary of the vacant lot, out toward the end of the Harwood House sidewalk at its junction with Fremont Street, where a left turn would head the Cowboy in the direction of the Third Street intersection. This would be the shortest route out of the danger zone for a man in Tom's position to take. At the point of this left turn toward Third Street, Tom McLaury would be menacingly close to Morgan Earp, and at a more opportune station to inflict the right-to-left, across the back of the shoulder wound, than Billy Clanton.

That, upon noting the assertion by Mrs. Wyatt Earp that it was actually Tom McLaury, and not Billy Clanton, who fired with deadly effect at Morgan, this author was astounded at first by such a claim. But eventually this author became an adherent to its defiant and bold contravention, in the face of the mass of opinion by Earp detractors who charge that McLaury was unarmed. These same Earp opponents were quick to discount the eyewitness testimonies of Tombstone residents, Messrs. J. B. W. Gardiner and Albert C. Bilicke, that Tom McLaury entered a butcher shop on Allen Street, just before the gunfight, and after a few minutes, came out with his right pants pocket a'bulge, as if a handgun was protruding therein. The same Earp bashers will mention instead, the sworn statement of Tombstone Saloon personage, Mr. Andy Mehan, that Tom had checked his firearm with the bartender just before the shoot-out.

That, further to the above, it seems pointless for Tom McLaury to obtain a pistol at the Allen Street butchery, only to turn around and leave it with saloon-keeper Mehan, just before the Fremont Street contest. Unless, Mehan, without knowing it, is referring to a pistol that Tom had left earlier in his safekeeping. Having been busted over the head by Wyatt Earp at approximately 1:00 p.m. on Fourth Street, then meeting the just-arrived-in-town Frank McLaury and Billy Clanton at Spangenburg's Gun Shop shortly thereafter, and being party to all of the confrontationist talk by Ike Clanton, (himself the earlier recipient of a head wound from Virgil), it would seem that the intuitive course of action for Tom McLaury would be to secure a weapon for self protection. Since saloonist J. H. Allman would also testify that Ike Clanton's six-shooter and Winchester were in his safekeeping, just before, and during the Fremont Street fight, it appears to be more than coincidental that, following the Spangenburg's visitation, Ike Clanton was reported as stopping in at an Allen Street Saloon, while Tom McLaury crossed the same street to enter Everhardy's Butcher Shop. Could these two confederates have access to other revolvers stashed around town? Even though the butcher at Everhardy's was to later deny in court that Tom had obtained a pistol from his market, what else was he to say, or do? The McLaury ranch was obviously a supplier of beef to the Everhardy's store. Since the cattle were probably stolen Mexican stock, at cut rate prices, a quid-pro-quo relationship, namely, 'you scratch my back, and I'll scratch yours', was bound to exist between the butcher and his supplier. (This does not preclude the possibility that at the same time Tom could have collected monies due his ranch for previously-sold cattle in that McLaury was found to have over two thousand dollars on his person when he died.)

That, this author contends that it was already a well-established alibi for both Ike Clanton and Tom McLaury to have claimed not to be armed, since their known weapons were being held by the two Tombstone saloon keepers previously mentioned. Eyewitnesses would report that Ike was denied a new weapon at Spangenburg's Gun Shop. Why push the issue? The gunsmith would have to testify to the truth, (if called upon), that Clanton tried to re-arm himself but was refused at this locality. Another strong vindication for Clanton. For Ike and Tom to travel from the Fourth Street gun shop to their Allen Street destinations, they would have had to pass Hafford's Corner at Fourth and Allen where the visibly heavy-armed Earps were headquartered. In the face of such real danger all around them, it is the belief of this author that Ike Clanton and Tom McLaury went to their Allen Street destinations to obtain firearms from sources that both men were confident would take such secrets to the grave.

That, having clandestinely re-armed, Ike and Tom then went to Fremont Street to the vacant lot, to join their pistol-packing brothers, with the expectation that they would encounter Doc Holliday at some point, thereby being presented with a first-hand opportunity to bushwhack the gambling dentist. (Doc's woman, 'Big Nosed' Kate Elder, would later give an account that Ike entered Fly's Rooming House earlier that day, armed with pistol and rifle, looking for Holliday.) The Cowboys would feel emboldened to settle scores with one more to their kind, namely, the controversial and sometimes rumored law-skirter himself, Doc Holliday, than to try to assassinate, in broad daylight, legitimate city Officers like Marshal Virgil Earp and his part-time replacement, brother, Wyatt.

That, assuming that Sheriff Behan, at some point, became aware of the covert acquisition of firearms on the part of Ike Clanton and Tom McLaury, it would then be to the same Sheriff Behan that this author would look as the 'early bird on the scene', (right after the shooting stopped), with the perfect opportunity to snatch up Tom's pistol, thereby protecting the illegal source of the weapon at Everhardy's Meat Market, as well as besmirching the Earps and Holliday as murderers of unarmed men near the O.K. Corral.

That, because Ike Clanton had successfully fled the area of the street brawl, his sidearm could have remained with him at all times, giving rise to the speculation that it was Ike who fired the shot....the distraction....from between the two Fly's buildings. If not, Ike could have handed the weapon to one of his Cowboy 'allies' in the rooming house, (as he ran through the place), so that if caught outside by the Earps, he, Ike, could continue to plead no firearms. In this event, one of his cohorts in the Fly's building could have used the six-gun to lay down a protective fire to cover Clanton's retreat. (Some Earp scholars actually attribute the source of the gunfire, the distraction, to Will 'Billy' Allen, shooting from the passage-way between the two Fly's buildings.)

THE WOUNDING OF VIRGIL EARP:

That, here again, this author is caused to take issue with the prevalent view that Billy Clanton was the triggerman who inflicted Virgil Earp's wound. The Marshal was standing to Billy's front, both men almost directly opposite of each other, with Billy ending up against the corner of the Harwood House, and Virgil just over the boundary between the vacant lot and the sidewalks. For Billy, from his position, to fire and hit Virgil in the lower leg, the bullet would have had to, in all probability, shatter the shin bone, or at least graze it, before perforating the flesh of the calf.

That, this writer understands that Marshal Earp's wound was to the right leg. To the calf. The slug entering from Virgil's right side, penetrating straight through the flesh of the calf, out the left side. The shin bone was undamaged. (To inflict such a close-to-the-ground wound, the triggerman, if standing erect, would have to shoot downward, a most unlikely scenario in this case, or, if crouching, i.e., shooting from under his horse's neck, the triggerman's upward mobility would be limited, leaving him with little choice but to fire a low-trajectory bullet straight at his victim's bottom limbs.)

That, while theorists who believe that it was Virgil who situated himself innermost in the vacant lot, (and not Wyatt, as claimed by this author), the same proponents would then abet their findings by stating that Billy would be at an oblique....a sort of right angle....to the Marshal. Hence, any shot from the youthful Clanton toward the lawman would have to be a north-south shot, (Billy's right, at Virgil's right), provided, however, that the City Marshal were looking straight ahead to the west, with his body in the same stance. Since this author believes that, in such an innermost position, Virgil would have had to turn slightly to his right in order to have initially addressed the Cowboy threesome of Tom McLaury, Billy Clanton, and Frank McLaury, in that order, (all three gunmen standing with their backs to the Harwood House), then, in such event, would Billy Clanton not have had a clean sideways shot into the fleshy part of Earp's right calf, let alone miss the shin bone entirely.

That, the foregoing assumption must now be taken, with Virgil Earp's testimony at the Wells Spicer hearing in November, 1881, when the Marshal revealed that he fired four pistol shots during the clamor, one at Frank McLaury, and three at Billy Clanton. Which prompts this author to raise the question that if Billy Clanton was not at the so-called right angle to deliver the shot through the flesh of Earp's right calf, then who was? The gunman would have had to be located on Fremont Street, the more eastward the better, so as to be on Virgil's right, to effectively inflict the wound as reported. The only member of the Cowboy crowd in such a position was Frank McLaury, seen by at least one eyewitness to be firing from under the neck of a horse....firing, this author believes....in the direction of Virgil and Wyatt Earp. Shooting toward the vacant lot.

That, it is appropriate to mention here that Mrs. 'Josie' Earp's account of the gun battle, attributes Virgil's wound to either Billy Clanton, OR TO FRANK McLAURY.

That, it is also timely to recount Tombstone Epitaph editor, John P. Clum's lengthy report of the gunfight that appeared in his newspaper the following day, October 27, 1881. Mr. Clum wrote, "Mr. Earp, (Virgil), says it was the first shot from Frank McLaury that hit him".

That, to the matter of the Marshal firing one of his four shots at Frank McLaury, this author can only hope to visualize the smoke-filled conditions within the vacant lot at the time. Explosion after deafening explosion of deadly guns all around the trap-like arena; the sounds of the wounded and dying; of yelping horses kicking violently; of blood gushing from fatal injuries; of suffocating powder fumes that burn the eyes to a blood red; the adrenaline; the horror of not knowing where the bullet with your name on it will come from. So, when you feel a .45 caliber slug whiz by your ear, or, if you are actually hit and nearly bowled over by the force of a shot from your enemy, there can be no luxury in such a gory environment to think about who your pistol should be pointed at. You shoot back. You react. You return fire at the man trying at that very moment to kill you. Get him or he will get you. Thus does this author opinionate that Virgil Earp fired at Frank McLaury because it was Frank, not Billy Clanton, who was the gun handler who caused the wound to the Marshal's right leg calf.

That, by the time Marshal Earp could thumb another shot at Frank McLaury across Fremont Street, the staccato of Billy Clanton's mortiferous fire was upon him. Get him, or he will get you. React. Return fire at the man who at that moment is trying to kill you. Kill him first. So it was that Virgil Earp now turned on the young Cowboy, and in the words of 'Josie' Earp, "finished off Billy".

WHEN TOM McLAURY FELL:

That, this author, after long and incisive deliberation of the available facts, and having recently been emboldened by the opinions of the two salient authors, (Messrs. Traywick and Boyer), is of the opinion that Tom McLaury could not have been shot, and have fallen, during the opening seconds of the Fremont Street tumult. Wyatt Earp described

Doc Holliday as the "quickest man" with a pistol he ever saw. No dispute here as to the speed with which Holliday could bring a six-shooter, knife, or shotgun, into play. The problem, as a number of Western historians will attest, is not with Doc's quickness, but with his accuracy. The speed-of-light Holliday was witnessed to have engaged in a number of shootings during his rambunctious career as a gambler-gunfighter during the 1870's and 1880's. But, on many of such occasions, Doc, while firing instantly and before his opponent could draw, did not actually kill his enemy. Holliday missed and winged his adversary more than he came near to ending his victim's life on earth. Contrary to the temptation to associate a high moral standard, a supreme self-control mechanism, if you will, to the alcohol-infested Holliday that would prompt him to incapacitate his antagonist rather than to snuff him out permanently, well, we can all dream on. When Doc Holliday pulled the trigger, it was for real. It was shoot to kill. And anyone with any smarts, who knew of Doc's real effectiveness as a shooter, and, who might have found himself in the vicinity of a Doc Holliday 'brouhaha', would show the most admirable acuity if he got the hell out of the area. You just never knew where a Doc Holliday bullet could end up.

That, and as will be shown later in this segment, it is to the aforestated rationale that this author attaches the belief that Doc Holliday did not shoot down Tom McLaury with the sawed-off shotgun during the initial moments of the fight.

That, the sworn testimony of dressmaker Ms. Addie Bourland, who saw the combatants approach each other just prior to the start of the gunfire, would immediately speak for this author's hypothesis. Ms. Bourland reported, "and a man with a long coat, (Holliday), walked up to the man holding the horse and put a pistol to his stomach, then stepped back two or three feet, and then the firing became general"....The unanimity of eyewitness accounts placed Doc at the outside of the Earp delegation, on Fremont Street, as the lawmen came up to the Cowboys. Likewise, the majority of reports describe Frank McLaury as holding one of the horses, and as being the member of the Cowboy group standing nearest to the street. At such close range even the spray-shooting Doc Holliday is given the benefit of all doubts. It was his bullet that struck Frank McLaury one inch left of the navel, which action then started the entire Fremont Street holocaust in earnest. From her strategic lookout in the milliner's shop opposite the vacant lot, scene of the upheaval, Ms. Bourland was later to remember the weapon being touted by Doc Holliday as "a very large pistol"

That, in fairness to those believers who vehemently insist that Doc Holliday disported the shotgun in the opening seconds, Ms. Bourland, in a manner of speaking, would seem to have likewise advanced their cause by her response to the examiner's queries during her testimony. When asked to describe the firearm held by Holliday, she said, "It was dark bronze"...."It was not a nickel-plated pistol".

What manner of gun be this?

Could the switch-hitting Mr. Holliday have actually flaunted two weapons at the same time during the instant the shooting started, namely, the sawed-off shotgun in the left hand

and the nickel-plated revolver in his right? No one would ever accuse Doc of lacking a sense of theatre when it opportuned. But the thought of the frail, sickly, one hundred-fifty pound Holliday, detonating a shotgun with his non-gun hand, without using all of his strength, (as flimsy as it was), to steady himself from the savage recoil, is a little too much for this author to accept. Even the most experienced shotmakers in heavy ordinance always try to 'let go' with both arms controlling their weapon, and with their feet firmly planted on the ground. (Nationally-recognized Tombstone author, Ben T. Traywick, opinionates that Ms. Bourland may have actually seen a part of the barrel of the sawed-off shotgun obtruding out of the left side of Holliday's coat.)

Besides, this author argues that Doc actually put the scatter-gun into play against Tom McLaury, and only against Tom McLaury, not at the beginning of the fight, but when the battle was already well underway. And that it was a six-gun shot from a Colt pistol, (Doc's), that critically wounded Frank McLaury during the first seconds of the armed clash.

That, if Doc Holliday did not use the shotgun to start the rumble on Fremont Street, then what would be the point to his openly exhibiting such an insidious weapon in the first place, when just minutes earlier Virgil Earp had asked Doc to hide the very same gun under his great coat? No question that the venomous Holliday was in a homicidal mode. But, such a state of mind may have only simmered within himself. (Holliday's ferocity might have also been realized by Morgan Earp, the latter equally quick-triggered that day.) The hidden rage in Mr. Holliday was believed to be in contrast to a more amiable state of mind on the part of Virgil Earp to attempt to disarm the Cowboys without bloodshed. Therefore, and in all probability, Doc and Virgil were at a sort of cross purposes before the shooting began. Doc knew it. He was not about to tip his hand to the unsuspecting Marshal, either. To do so might have brought strong forebodings from Virgil that would deny Holliday the showdown he was hell-bent on starting with the Clantons and McLaurys, law or no law.

That, to Addie Bourland's courtroom attestations is attributed the suggestion that Doc Holliday's nickel-plated sidearm could have appeared to be a "dark bronze" color under the light of that overcast cold October afternoon from her post across the street. Possible. (Tombstone resident-historian, Ben T. Traywick, claims to have re-enacted this scene by holding a nickel-plated metallic object, and having the same viewed from the exact distance across Fremont Street occupied by the said Ms. Bourland from her position in the Milliner's Shop. Mr. Traywick states that the color of the weapon would appear to be bronze depending on the light of day.)

That, could the "very large pistol" alleged by Ms. Bourland, have been a seven-and-a-half inch barrel Colt .45 Peacemaker; or a Smith and Wesson .44 caliber, with an even greater length? Unlikely. Again, the skinny weakened physical countenance of the diseased Doc Holliday must be considered. Such a man, (or what was left of him), was not apt to favor anything large, or heavy, in weaponry. He would want something as light as possible that he could handle, and swiftly catapult into action. Further, he would prefer a pistol that could easily be secreted under his frock coat, either in a scabbard at his hip, or in a vest pocket. Certain students of Doc Holliday's arsenal of death-spitting artillery, (including Tombstone historical expert, Ben T. Traywick), stand in avowal that the alcoholic shooter used a four-and-three-quarter inch barreled .38, and/or, .41 caliber nickel-plated, ivory handled Colt pistol. Nothing larger or weightier, considering he could hardly lift what he had, to begin with. This type of short-snouted 'heater' is obviously not the character of revolver referred to by depositor Addie Bourland.

That, the author now raises the obvious. Could Ms. Bourland have deliberately muddied the waters, so to speak? After all, to proclaim that Doc Holliday used the nickel-plated pistol, at the start of the proceedings, might lend credence to the prosecution's charge that Doc, without provocation or clear threat from the Cowboys, opened fire with such a repeater and 'murdered' Frank McLaury. Likewise, Morgan Earp 'murdered' Billy Clanton. Mrs. 'Josie' Earp, in the book I Married Wyatt Earp, claims that it was both her husband and his brother Virgil who actually covered up during the Wells Spicer hearing following the street fight. Both Wyatt and Virgil did so to protect Morgan and Doc, with Wyatt, for starters, assuming the direct role of having administered the shot into Frank McLaury. The Earps would then assert that Doc carried the shotgun from the beginning, but only entered the deadly imbroglio when the firing became general, and then, in defense against a threat to the Official's party from Tom McLaury. (Since it was a pivotal strategem of the prosecutor to target Doc Holliday and Morgan Earp as the two hotheads of questionable legal standing, who, in fact, provoked the blood bath on Fremont Street, it then became paramount for the defense to counter with a sort of lesser-of-two-evils rebuttal. Namely, that it would befall the broad shoulders of the two recognized and legitimate law authorities in Tombstone, Virgil and Wyatt Earp, to step forward and to take responsibility. They would do so by castigating the Cowboys as initially refusing to obey the Marshal's order to give up their arms. Instead, Billy Clanton and Frank McLaury drew their pistols and therefore were blamed for starting the bloody mess....or so the two Earp law men would claim in their courtroom statements.)

That, in light of the aforestated delineations, one would have to believe it possible that Ms. Bourland was an Earp loyalist, all along, who, by clouding the issue as to the type of weapon conveyed by Doc Holliday in the first seconds of the shoot-out, would thusly be supporting the case for the defense, resulting in the exculpation of the Earps from the charge of capital murder. To this probability, the reader of these contents is reminded of that prideful revelation in Mrs. 'Josie' Earp's life story, when she speaks of Addie Bourland as...."my good friend". And now, to finish the subject of when Tom McLaury fell.

That, Tom McLaury, according to Tombstone Coroner, H. M. Mathews, was killed by a cluster of twelve wounds, believed to be buckshot, in the rib cage on the right side of the body. Since the only man in the Marshal's coterie who held the shotgun was the obstreperous Doc Holliday, and, there not being reported any other death-dealing pistol shot wounds on McLaury's body, it would seem tantamount to mental derangement to reach any other conclusion but that Tom McLaury was killed by a buckshot blast from the shotgun held, and fired by Doc Holliday.

That, were Doc to have turned the said shotgun toward Tom McLaury immediately after inflicting the stomach wound on Tom's older brother, Frank, then, in such event, Holliday would have had to fire one pistol shot into Frank, holstered the pistol, drawn the shotgun for which action Doc would have needed to use both of his hands, and then, as anti-Earp cynics would have us believe, have shot Tom within, or near, the vacant lot enclosure, or, might even have 'caught' Tom out in the street making a run for Third and Fremont to the west, DURING THE OPENING SECONDS OF THE STREET FIGHT. In all of the noise and confusion that must have permeated the calamitous scene at the time, it befuddles this author to picture the long-coated Holliday exchanging armaments out in the street between pistol....shotgun....and pistol....although the possibility of such a quick draw accomplishment is not to be questioned, where Doc is concerned, for it really did happen that way! It is not the actual 'switch' of weapons under scrutiny here, as it is more the exact moment in time that such a Houdini-like shift took place. With bullets about to wreak death upon him at any moment, why expend the priceless seconds, (wearing a cumbersome coat), to change artillery, when, already armed with his trusted short-barreled Colt in hand, Doc could have used the same weapon to keep 'popping off' at Tom McLaury? In such a multi-party shoot-out, is it one's instinct to first shoot to kill? Or is it to do so with the selectivity of weapons in mind, assuming of course, that in such a hot environment one even has the luxury to think about it, let alone do it?

That, to the riddles just posed concerning the point in time in the Fremont Street turmoil that Tom McLaury was killed should be added the question of whether Doc Holliday, callous shootist or not, would have turned his shotgun toward Tom McLaury, while he, (Tom), was still inside, or in the line of fire of the vacant lot. This could indeed be a reckless undertaking. It is okay to turn a shrapnel-spitting weapon on your enemies provided that your friends are not around. Buckshot pellets are not known to discriminate. This author has tried to put himself in the place, and in the mind-set, of such rapid-fire shooting as would have characterized the Fremont Street mayhem on October 26, 1881. In so doing, a number of accomplished pistol handlers have sided with my conclusion that the tendency, under such pressure, (when Doc opened fire on Frank McLaury, and then, with Morgan Earp, had to guard against McLaury's onrushing horse out in the street, plus the still dangerous Frank himself), would be to stick with the weapon that you have out at the time, and to which you feel most confident and skilled. When you have exhausted its ammunition, you reach for another, assuming that a back-up firearm is in your possession.

That, this author rejects the notion that an unarmed Tom McLaury was 'murdered' by Doc Holliday in the opening moments of the battle. Under such a scenario, McLaury would have had to IMMEDIATELY make his way out of the vacant lot with his terrorized horse in tow, past the wounded Billy Clanton, thereby placing Tom within proximity of Holliday, who would have had to instantly swap weapons, all of such simultaneous movements to enable the eventual outcome, namely, that Doc annihilated Tom with the shotgun. As a matter of fact, it just about happened that way. But not so early in the gunfight. Later. Instead, this author believes that Doc, true to such instincts, stayed with his favorite nickel-plated revolver in order to attempt to finish Frank McLaury; and to nail his sworn enemy, Ike Clanton, as he, (Doc), spied Clanton running away from the scene. After having fired four pistol shots, Doc then became enraged at the sight of Tom McLaury's shot-in-the-back of Morgan Earp, (a very special Earp to Doc Holliday). Tom, firing over the horse's saddle and from behind it, was well protected, and successfully edging his way out of the area. With such a formidable target to stop, and with just one cartridge left in his pistol, now was the time when Doc HAD to change weapons. You do not elect to stop an armed man and a big horse with a single pistol shot if you also happen to have a double-barreled shotgun on your person. As it developed and at the exact same time, Wyatt Earp, shooting from within the vacant lot, winged Tom's horse. The animal broke away from its handler, exposing him to certain death at the hands of Doc Holliday. Tom McLaury subsequently collapsed at the intersection of Fremont and Third Streets.

EYEWITNESS REPORTS:

That, this author wishes to now direct his comments at some of the courtroom testimony by eyewitnesses to the gunfight, particularly as such reports would tend to enhance the author's version of the events. For example, the preceding subject, dealing with the matter of the time when Tom McLaury would have been attacked by Doc Holliday, has some corroborative reference in the sworn testimony of a Mr. B. H. Fallehy at the Coroner's Inquest on October 29, 1881. Mr. Fallehy states, in part, "I saw Doc Holliday in the middle of the street....Holliday also fired at the man behind the horse, AND FIRING AT A MAN, WHO RAN BY HIM ON THE OPPOSITE SIDE OF THE STREET"....(The capitalized words in Mr. Fallehy's account is this author's work and is an attempt to emphasize the relevance of this statement to the depiction of hostilities herein.) The man reported as, "who ran by him on the opposite side of the street", is Tom McLaury, who, in the opinion of this author, has just lost his horse; has taken the fatal charge of buckshot to his right side from Holliday; and is now, by virtue of the force of the impact from Doc's powerful weapon, in the final anguish of stumbling toward the intersection of Third and Fremont Streets, where he will fall. Reference to "the opposite side of the street", by eyewitness Fallehy, is understandable when one takes into account that the other McLaury, Frank, himself critically wounded, is hanging onto his horse, at the same time using the animal for protection, and too, is heading across Fremont Street to the boardwalks in front of the northside buildings. In other words, the two wounded McLaury brothers, to a viewer on Fremont Street looking from east to west, (as was the position of onlooker Fallehy at the time), would appear to be at opposite sides of the street. That is almost how the two McLaurys fell....Tom toward the south side at the corner of Fremont and Third....and Frank on the northside, obliquely across from the vacant lot fronting Fly's Boarding House.

That, while we Tombstone enthusiasts look to eyewitness accounts to give us a sort of a 'flash bulb picture' of the happenings taking place at that exact moment in time so that we can put such evidence to use to accredit our rendition of events, we must, at the same time, learn how to interpret such reports. There is little question that sentiments in Tombstone were divided along factional lines at the time. You were either pro-Earp or pro-Cowboy. It seems difficult to imagine one living in that locality without being pressed into declaring a public or private position in support of one or the other group. Hence, as emotions reached a peak following the Fremont Street uproar, it was inevitable that eyewitnesses who were called to testify as to their version of the activities, would lend an extra emphasis here; a nuance there; a lucid recollection when such would advantage the position of whomever the witness happened to favor; or even a sudden lapse of memory if by such sufferance the fortunes of the favored party would be upheld.

That, to elucidate this author's position concerning the interpretation of eyewitness reports, let us look at several specific excerpts pertinent to the subject hereto. In the feature story of the gunfight, carried by The Tombstone Epitaph newspaper the next day, October 27, 1881, witness R. F. Coleman was quoted extensively. He said, in part, "Bill Clanton fell next, raised to fire again when Mr. Fly took his revolver from him. Frank McLaury ran a few rods and fell".... Whoa. Just a minute Mr. Coleman. Both Billy Clanton and Frank McLaury were first to be hit when the shooting started. They were the last to fall. When they did, the fight was over. Meanwhile, 'the most famous thirty seconds in the history of the Old West' just happened to have transpired between the two occurrences. One would hope that Mr. Coleman would have been encouraged to keep his remarks to more of a 'blow-by-blow' description of the events, rather than to have co-mingled his comments by what he actually saw at the time, with what he came to know was the final outcome.

That, let us now examine more closely the previously-utilized reportage concerning eyewitness Mrs. J. C. Colyer, who viewed the commotion while sitting in a wagon parked in front of the Post Office on the corner of Fourth and Fremont Streets. Mrs. Colyer said, in part, "....one of the Cowboys, after he had been shot three times, raised himself on his elbow and shot one of the Officers and fell back dead. Another used his horse as a barricade and shot under its neck". Here we go again. A person with all good intentions, and languishing for the moment in the fame and attraction unique to a real eyewitness in those days, gives a newspaper interview. In so doing, she juggles her report to include not only part of an actual event as she saw it, but also the end result of the entire drama, as told to her after the fact. From her position, there was no way, (in the opinion of this author), that Mrs. Colyer could have seen all of Billy Clanton's movements, let alone have discerned, (from such a distance), that there were three wounds on the rugged Cowboy. But, it is obvious that Mrs. Colyer learned about the specific number and nature of Billy's wounds after the gunfight from the published coroner's report, courtroom testimony, or from other Tombstone hearsay, and, combined with her presence in the area on that fateful day, Mrs. Colyer was to become an instant celebrity. This author stands by his conclusion that Billy Clanton, hit three times, namely, left chest, right side of body, and right hand, (plus a perforation near the knee of the right pants leg in the cloth only, not a penetration of flesh), did not inflict the leg wound on Virgil Earp, for reasons previously explained. The Marshal's assailant must have been Frank McLaury. However, and while on the subject of Frank, the same Mrs. Colyer refers to this scene, "Another used his horse as a barricade and shot under its neck". This author finds credibility in this particular report because other onlookers located at various outlets along Fremont Street during the gunfire were to report Frank McLaury's presence on the same street with a horse. Mrs. Colyer could see Frank in the middle of the street from her vantage point. That she reported that Frank had fired under the neck of his horse is in keeping with this author's assertion that it was from such a position that McLaury hit Virgil Earp in the calf of his right leg.

That, finally, and on the subject of eyewitness reports of the Tombstone Street fight, let us return to the most interesting of such accounts to this author, namely, the heretofore quoted Mr. C. H. Light, who observed the action from his quarters at the Aztec Rooming House on Fremont and Third Streets. Mr. Light's story is worth repeating here, "saw several men in the act of shooting....Tom McLaury reel and fall on the corner of Fremont and Third....observed three men, (of the Earp party), standing at an angle about ten or fifteen feet apart, about the center of the street, facing Fly's Photograph Gallery....saw another man - Billy Clanton - leaning against the corner of the Harwood House, and a man with a horse - Frank McLaury".

This author would be inclined to rest his case on the content of this, (C. H. Light's), account of the street fight by citing the "three men of the Earp party facing Fly's house" as dramatic evidence of the so-called 'distraction' from the rear of the main Fly's building. However, the fact that Mr. Light implies, in the same report, that Tom McLaury had just fallen on the corner of Fremont and Third Streets, would negate this author's sequence of events as having McLaury actually shot some seconds after the distraction. Was this a 'flash bulb' like depiction of the events that were taking place at that exact point in time? Had McLaury just been felled at the time that three of the Earp group were facing toward Fly's hostelry?

Or, is this not another case where an eyewitness to one part of an event tries to give a blow-by-blow account of that part, but, to appear authoritative as to the outcome of the whole of such an historic experience, the witness juxtaposes what he saw with what he knows was the final disposition? A researcher might be satisfied with this type of overview. But to someone trying to reconstruct this most epic of Frontier episodes, to test the long-held belief that the Tombstone street fight "lasted thirty seconds, with about thirty shots fired", such a task can indeed prove beguiling.

By reason of these notes and accompanying illustrations, this author presents, with humility, his shot-by-shot, second-by-second, analysis of The Street Fight in Tombstone, Near the O.K. Corral, "all thirty seconds of it, with about thirty shots fired", just the way it might have happened, a long time ago, as told to me by that venerable old-timer in Tombstone.

As I remember him, I am inclined toward profound sentiment. For I realize that in this age of fast-paced events, and of modern technology, there are but only a few places that remain where the old-timers may gather to talk about the old days, and the old ways, of that most redoubtable by-gone era of our nation's history. Tombstone is one of them.

EDITED CORRESPONDENCE BETWEEN THE AUTHOR AND TOMBSTONE RESIDENT-HISTORIAN AND EARP RESEARCHER, BEN T. TRAYWICK

June 20, 1991

MR. BEN T. TRAYWICK

Re: Street Fight in Tombstone, Near the O.K. Corral

Dear Ben:

Note: Introductory paragraph(s) and preamble deleted.

1. The date that Billy Claibourne met his death in Tombstone, at the hands of 'Buckskin' Frank Leslie, has been corrected to November 14, 1882, via a pistol shot to the side, (instead of on November 4th, via a bullet in the chest).

2. The age of Doc Holliday at the time of his death in Glenwood Springs, Colorado, in 1887, has been revised, namely, from 35 to 36 years.

3. Doc Holliday's personal arsenal of weaponry, which you describe as 'Thunder and Lightning'; were reportedly two Colt pistols, one a .38 caliber, and the other a .41 caliber, one or both believed to be of four-and-three-quarter inch barrel length(s). This correction has been duly noted in the finished text.

4. Wyatt Earp's position as Acting Marshal, at the time of his courtroom testimony in November, 1881, has been corrected in favor of no position at all, in that Virgil was removed from his post after the October 26, 1881 street fight, and temporarily replaced by James Flynn. Thank you for this redress.

5. The fact that John H. Behan had not yet been appointed Cochise County Sheriff at the time that he was living with Josephine Sarah Marcus, (1880), has been amended accordingly. (Behan assumed office the following year, February 1, 1881.)

6. Your strong assertion that no clear incontrovertible evidence exists to support the claim that the so-called 'Buntline Special' revolver, with twelve (12) inch barrel, was ever disported by Wyatt Earp during the Tombstone gunfight on October 26, 1881, is hereby acknowledged. (If the undersigned reads your thoughts accurately on this matter, you would seem to doubt the very existence of such a gun, in the first place.) This author defers

to your expertise. The pistol wielded by Mr. Earp in my book now alludes to a .45 caliber Colt; seven-and-one-half inch barrel; blue steel; well worn; wood-handled; single action, six-shooter; otherwise known as 'Peacemaker', but, which the slang of the Frontier more freely referred to as a 'Hog-leg'.

7.   The error in my manuscript wherein Cowboy sidekick, Wesley 'Wes' Fuller, was called 'West' Fuller was typographical. The correction has been effected. Much obliged.

8.   The undersigned considers your personal observations as to what Ms. Addie Bourland might have seen from her vantage point across from the shoot-out enclosure, to be important enough to include in the 'Author's Working Notes' section of the book. For example, you seem to have proven to yourself by actually re-enacting the scene, (and distance), in Tombstone, that a nickel-plated metallic object, when viewed from Ms. Bourland's station opposite of Fly's Rooming House, could appear to be 'bronze' in color, under certain conditions of daylight. In furtherance to this subject, your guess that Ms. Bourland could have also seen part of the double-barreled sawed-off (bronze) shotgun sticking out from under the left side of Doc Holliday's great coat, as the confronters came face-to-face, has also been cited.

9.   As to the exact words attributed to Virgil Earp at the time he noticed, with incredulity, that his brother, Morgan, and Doc Holliday had cocked their pistols to open fire on the Cowboys, thereby starting the bloody affray on Fremont Street, this author accepts your critique to the language, thusly, "Hold....I don't mean that".

Note: Closing paragraph(s) and felicitations deleted.

Michael M. Hickey

June 13, 1991

MR. BEN T. TRAYWICK

Re: <u>Street Fight in Tombstone, Near the O.K. Corral</u>

Dear Ben:

Note: Introductory paragraph(s) and preamble deleted.

*   As to the number of shots fired, and by whom, let me preface my comments by emphasizing your theory that the historic confrontation was an accident. If so, it is unlikely that the combatants would have 'loaded up' prior to the gunfire by stocking their revolvers with six (6) bullets. The undersigned assumes that those so armed, carried the cautionary five (5) slugs in their chamber, with 'one empty' against the hammer of their pistol. With this thought foremost in mind, here goes.

*   Wyatt Earp fired five (5) shots. The first was an accidental discharge in the opening seconds, when struggling with Ike Clanton, which bullet probably was the one that Billy Claibourne later testified struck his pants leg, near the knee. Wyatt's second shot was to his rear at a 'distraction' between the two Fly's buildings. His third and fourth shots were at Tom McLaury, (behind Billy Clanton's horse), the first of the two grazing the animal, to the extent that it panicked and ran, exposing Tom to Doc Holliday's sawed-off shotgun. Wyatt's last bullet was intended for Frank McLaury out on Fremont Street at the end of the shooting; at the very same moment that the said McLaury was firing at Doc Holliday; with both Doc and Morgan Earp firing back at him, (Frank McLaury). The fight ended after this.

*   Now Ben, hold onto your seat. The undersigned contends that although having fired five times, (literally emptying his six shooter), Wyatt Earp did not hit anyone....wound anyone....or, did not kill anyone! That's right. In this most heralded incident in Wyatt's illustrious career, he missed, except for winging Tom McLaury's horse. By being farthest in, (south), in the vacant lot, Earp, in the opinion of the undersigned, was somewhat removed from the more direct exchanges occurring to his right and out in the street, between Virgil against Billy Clanton; Tom McLaury, who almost from the commencement of the shooting headed speedily with the horse away from Wyatt toward Fremont Street and to Doc Holliday and out of the area of the enclosure; and Doc Holliday and Morgan Earp out in the street engaged with Frank McLaury.

*   Because Wyatt was, in a way, isolated, and deepest in the vacant lot, he would have to restrain his shooting so that he would not hit anyone of his own party, then in the general line of his fire to the right, (north), toward the street. This was a disadvantage only from the standpoint of not scoring any hits on the Cowboys. The good thing about his position was that Wyatt was not a conspicuous, tempting, 'point blank target', for the Cowboys to hit, either. Hence, only Wyatt Earp emerged from the violent melee, unscathed.

*   The undersigned takes Virgil Earp at his testimony. He fired four (4) times. Once at Frank McLaury, and his last three (3) shots in a murderous one-on-one exchange with Billy Clanton.

*   Morgan Earp emptied his pistol. His first two bullets struck home at Billy Clanton in the Cowboy's left chest, and right wrist. Morg also loosed two shots at Frank McLaury behind the horse on Fremont Street. Both missed. But Morgan's last shot did not. It is believed by the undersigned to be the 'killing shot', below the right ear, that finished Frank and brought a halt to the hostilities.

*   Doc Holliday fired seven (7) times, five (5) handgun shots, plus two (2) shotgun discharges, the latter with deadly effect at Tom McLaury. Doc's first pistol shot opened the street fight and pierced Frank McLaury's abdomen, near the navel. Holliday fired again at Frank McLaury behind the horse. Missed. Then he, (Doc), spotted Ike Clanton making a break through the front door of Fly's Rooming House, and unloosed two quick shots at Ike, both misses. Doc's final bullet was directed at Frank McLaury in a last second, four-way exchange between Holliday, Wyatt and Morgan Earp, and Frank himself, that resulted in Doc sustaining a slight wound to his hip. Frank took Morgan's bullet in his cranium and died almost immediately.

*   On the Cowboy side, Billy Clanton emptied his revolver, but did not hit anyone, (asserts the undersigned), despite massive claims to the contrary.

*   Frank McLaury, according to Coroner Matthews, had two (2) unexpelled cartridges in the chamber of his weapon. That means he fired three (3) times. The first, in the direction of Virgil and Wyatt Earp in front of him, in the vacant lot, which slug tore through Virgil's right calf. McLaury's second shot, in the same direction, missed. His third, inflicted a slight flesh wound on Doc Holliday's hip, on the left side, as previously stated.

*   Ike Clanton did not fire any shots while within the vacant lot. This is not to say that he was not armed. Moreover, he could have had a direct hand in 'the distraction' between the two Fly's buildings claimed by Josie Earp in Glenn G. Boyer's, <u>I Married Wyatt Earp</u>.

*   Billy Claibourne did not fire any shots while within the vacant lot.

*   The undersigned subscribes to the Earp party's original allegation that Tom McLaury was armed, after all, and fired two (2) shots with a pistol over the saddle, (not under the neck), of Billy Clanton's horse. One missed. One hit. Morgan Earp took the second bullet in his right shoulder, across the back, exiting the left. Of all the debate pertaining to who shot who, and when, the most perplexing to the undersigned is the just-mentioned Tom McLaury scenario. For the life of me, I cannot find a clear-cut eyewitness report that factually, or even circumstantially, proves that Tom was Morgan's assailant. While it is tempting to cite Mrs. J. C. Colyer's account of "Another used his horse as a barricade and shot under its neck", still, this author accepts this attacker as not Tom, but his older brother Frank, firing from under his horse's neck out in the middle of Fremont Street, where eyewitness Colyer would be more apt to see him engaged in such an uncommon act from her vantage point.

But, if one is to find substance in Josie Earp's 'expose', about what actually happened in the 30-second fracas, including who did what to whom, then, the natural flow of events thereto, combined with the position the antagonists HAD TO BE STANDING IN TO HAVE BEEN WOUNDED IN THE MANNER, AND FROM THE DIRECTION ATTESTED BY THE INJURED PARTIES THEMSELVES, AND FROM THE CORONER'S REPORT, would speak strongly for the Tom McLaury triggerman theory. It was certainly possible. The more I thought about it, the more it seemed even probable.

The answer to this tantalizing question may be found in the testimony of that often accused two-faced rattlesnake, Sheriff John H. Behan. He alleged that he put his arm around Ike Clanton's waist and found that he, (Ike), was not armed. Then Behan said, "Tom McLaury pulled his coat open and showed that he was not armed". In other words, Behan searched Ike Clanton and definitely pronounced the braggart Cowboy leader to be without a firearm. But he does not seem to have done the same with Tom. Instead, he, (Behan), seems to have taken Tom at his word.

Again, Behan testified, "When I left the Clanton party to meet the Earps I was satisfied that Ike Clanton and Tom McLaury had no arms". But, then the Sheriff was asked if Ike and Tom could have had arms without him, (Behan), knowing it. His reply is most intriguing, "Ike Clanton could not have had arms and I not know it. TOM McLAURY MIGHT HAVE HAD A PISTOL SHOVED IN THE WAIST OF HIS PANTS AND I NOT KNOWN IT".

Ike Clanton was 'dead in the water' from a number of eyewitness reports that he was armed and threatening the Earps prior to the gunfight. Sheriff Behan HAD to testify that Ike was unarmed at the time of the shooting, truth, or no truth. The simple fact is that Clanton would need every bit of a defense to counter the overwhelming evidence that he was the cause of the mayhem by virtue of his drunken bravado, and by his brandishment of a rifle and a pistol on the streets earlier in the day.

But, under no such obligation to perjure himself, if necessary, was Sheriff Behan where Tom McLaury was concerned. Why didn't Mr. Behan state unequivocally that Tom, too, was unarmed? Behan knew that there were eyewitnesses who would assert that McLaury had acquired a pistol just before the street fight from a butcher's shop on Allen Street, and that he, (Behan), had better 'cover his tracks'. There were no such eyewitnesses to claim that Ike Clanton had re-armed himself. The Sheriff could feel safe and secure to declare Clanton as unarmed, without claims to the contrary. (Even the Earps would not press this issue, at the Wells Spicer trial that followed the street fight, where Ike Clanton was concerned.)

To wit, if there is no fear of an eyewitness to report to the contrary, then it can even be 'screamed from the highest mountain' that Ike Clanton was definitely not armed. But, if one knows for a fact that Tom McLaury carried a sidearm, and that there would be testimony from witnesses to such effect, then, one had better hedge their bets, lest it be proven that one be a perjurer. Of course, if one just happened to have been first on the scene, (following the shooting), to have secreted away Tom's pistol in order to besmirch the reputations of the Earps and Doc Holliday so as to cast blame on them for murdering an unarmed man, (Tom McLaury), then, this too can provide one with the advantage of being ambivalent in courtroom testimony. Now, the onus is on those who claim that Tom was carrying a pistol, and that with it, he shot Morgan Earp, to prove such a claim by producing the pistol itself! How subtle the turn of suspicion can be in such a case. Who is more apt to be considered as guilty? Those who say that Tom claimed to be unarmed, but could have been? Or those who charge that not only was Tom armed, but he shot and wounded Morgan Earp, but no weapon can be produced to back up such an accusation? Meanwhile, Tom was blown to pieces by a sawed-off, double-barreled shotgun, touted by Doc Holliday. With no weapon found on, or near, his body, (McLaury's), most people would be inclined to conclude that a cold-blooded murder was committed.

*   Are you still sitting down, Ben? Because here comes another kicker. This author finds some validity in the claims that the Cowboys did not open fire at first, despite being assaulted by a fusillade from Doc Holliday and Morgan Earp. The Cowboys actually started to shoot back, only after about ten (10) shots had first been fired, (including two discharges from Wyatt's and Billy Clanton's guns). There is sizeable testimony to this effect. But the undersigned was not swayed by such reports. The fact is that the Cowboys could not have fired back in the opening seconds, by virtue of their crippling wounds, the two startled horses concealing three of the rustlers, (Billy Clanton, Tom and Frank McLaury), and that two of their group, Ike Clanton and Billy Claibourne, bolted away from the scene and were not even shooters in the vacant lot to begin with.

Note: Closing paragraph(s) and felicitations deleted.

Michael M. Hickey

June 11, 1991

MR. BEN T. TRAYWICK

Re: <u>Street Fight in Tombstone, Near the O.K. Corral</u>

Dear Ben:

As this author prepares to mail a copy of the first-draft manuscript to you, containing his rendition of the aforereferenced historical event, allow me to provide this background delineation concerning the revelations in Glenn G. Boyer's important book, <u>I Married Wyatt Earp</u>, the recollections and the memoirs of Earp's third wife, Josephine Sarah Marcus 'Josie' Earp:

1.   For almost a century, researchers and scholars in 'Earpiana', and particularly in that much-storied facet of the career of the Earps in Tombstone, namely, the gunfight near the O.K. Corral, had only the sworn eyewitness testimonies at the Judge Wells Spicer hearing; the Coroner's Report; newspaper accounts; and hearsay passed down from generations of descendants of the famed Fremont Street confrontation, and from citizens and ranchers who lived in Tombstone and in the surrounding environs, from which to make their judgements, and to base their analysis as to who stood where, and who shot who. Expert opinion had to be markedly divided, in that the aforementioned eyewitness reports and courtroom statements were not only diverse, and conflicting, but, in most cases were spawned from personal loyalties, or animosities, depending on how a particular respondent felt about the Earps or the Cowboys, at the time.

2.   There is no clear 'trail of evidence' in the records that have been preserved over the past 110 years concerning the Fremont Street shooting, that can answer all of the tough questions as to who fired the bullets that killed or wounded so-and-so, and from what position were such shots fired. To rely on the statements of the Judge Spicer witnesses would still leave the big pieces to the puzzle unanswered. For example, one who really deciphers Wyatt Earp's testimony cannot help but be impressed by Earp's self-control under fire, that in the face of death and destruction everywhere, still, he was of the presence of mind, to discern that he should shoot first at Frank McLaury than at Billy Clanton, the latter who was also, according to Wyatt, in the act of pulling his pistol. To have Earp tell it, the Cowboys started to draw their weapons upon Virgil's demand to surrender, causing Wyatt to decide that it would be to Frank McLaury that he would direct his initial shot. Wow. Talk about Mr. Cool.

3.   Yet, there is also the preponderance of eyewitness accounts, not only from the Cowboys and from their sympathizers, but from other Tombstone citizens and bystanders as well, that it was the Earp party that actually started the shooting, with Doc Holliday and Morgan Earp opening fire on Frank McLaury and Billy Clanton respectively. That it was Doc,

not Wyatt, who hit McLaury in the stomach. And, it was Morgan's first two shots that crippled Billy Clanton. If you subscribe to this latter viewpoint, then it makes sense to also support the logic that Frank and Billy were standing to the northern extremity of the group of Cowboys, with Billy near the Fremont Street corner of the Harwood House, and Frank outside of him, toward the end of the boardwalks, almost on the main street. In other words, to hold to the assumption that Doc Holliday wounded Frank McLaury, and that Morgan Earp did likewise to Billy Clanton, would endorse the actual diagram of the positions of the combatants that was used as a reference during the Wells Spicer hearing. Such a chart showed, reading left to right, (south to north), that Tom McLaury, Billy Clanton, and Frank McLaury were standing with their backs to the Harwood House.

4.   Now, let us again take Wyatt Earp's side of the story. He testified, "....we came upon them close, Frank McLaury, Tom McLaury, and Billy Clanton, standing all in a row against the east side of the building on the opposite side of the vacant place...". Of course Wyatt does not specifically state that the three Cowboys were standing, from his line of sight, reading left to right, (south to north), Frank and Tom McLaury and Billy Clanton. He only says that the two McLaurys and young Billy stood "all in a row" against the building. By modern day interpretation, however, this would mean....left to right....as Earp saw them....Frank, Tom, and Billy, in that order. If you believe Wyatt's account of the gun battle, he could see Billy draw a pistol along with Frank McLaury, but he, (Earp), opted to shoot at Frank first, because McLaury was perceived to be the more dangerous gun handler of the two. Immediately Earp supporters would leap to this version as the 'truth, the whole truth, and nothing but the truth', because that would put Frank opposite Wyatt, and in the 'proper' position to take Earp's bullet to the stomach. Otherwise, Wyatt would have had to shoot across his own party, to his right, toward the road to get at Frank McLaury, who, according to the Cowboys' version of the opening events, was standing on the Fremont Street side of their group.

5.   It would appear that even the highly respected Earp authority, Alford E. Turner, was to adhere to Wyatt's rendition, as just described. For, in the illustrations contained in his book, The Earps Talk, Mr. Turner has Wyatt standing innermost in the vacant lot, with Virgil to his right, followed by Morgan and Doc Holliday, in that order. Mr. Turner denotes Frank McLaury across from Wyatt inside the lot, and not out toward the street. This author agrees with writer Turner's positioning of the Earps, but not with that reported for Frank McLaury. For thirty years this particular matter has troubled the undersigned. Something did not add up. How is it possible that witnesses would claim to see Frank McLaury, with horse, in the street, almost instantly upon hearing the first gunshots? How could Frank make his way out of the inside of the vacant lot, that fast, without at least knocking someone over in the cramped enclosure with nine men and two horses, (including Frank's), on his way out of the area?

6.   Why would witness Addie Bourland, from her dress shop diagonally across from the vacant lot, specifically mention Doc Holliday as walking "up to the man holding the horse and put a pistol to his stomach, then stepped back two or three feet and then the firing became general"? Ms. Bourland could have pin-pointed Wyatt, Virgil, or Morgan for that

matter. But, instead, she described Doc Holliday. Why? Was it because Doc was furthest out from the rest of the Earps, on the street, closest therefore to observer Bourland, threatening Frank McLaury, who, had to also be standing nearest to Fremont Street, and not inside of the lot?

Is it not the natural tendency for one to remember, and to report first, what was nearest and most vivid when viewing a multi-person scene of the type then beheld by Ms. Bourland from her vantage point across the street? If so, then no one can fault the presumption that Doc Holliday opposed Frank McLaury at close range, these two shootists being the members of their respective parties that stood outermost from the vacant lot. Now, the overwhelming testimony that attributed Frank McLaury's belly wound to Doc Holliday's nickel-plated pistol begins to make sense, especially when you also recall the number of accounts that put McLaury out on Fremont Street with his horse, almost immediately after the first shots were fired. And since Morgan Earp was reported in virtually every eyewitness account to be standing next to Doc, and likewise Billy Clanton was described in most, if not all depictions, as standing near to the Fremont Street corner of the Harwood House, it does not take a genius to figure out that it was Morg and Doc who stood adversarial to Billy Clanton and to Frank McLaury, on the street side of their respective groups.

And now, briefly, let us consider some sworn eyewitness testimony that supports this author's belief that it was Frank McLaury who stood farthest out from the group of Cowboys, toward the street:

"The first thing the Cowboys did when the other party, (Earps), approached them was to raise up and come out to meet them from the side of the house....One man, (Frank McLaury), was holding a horse, the man with the horse standing outside."

- Ms. Addie Bourland

"When firing commenced Frank McLaury was standing by and holding a horse."

- Wesley 'Wes' Fuller

"Frank McLaury had hold of a horse about the corner of the post."

- William 'Billy The Kid' Claibourne

"I saw Frank McLaury on the sidewalk a few feet from the line of the front of the lot."

- Sheriff John H. Behan

7.   But, it was to Glenn G. Boyer's book, I Married Wyatt Earp, that this author's shot-by-shot, second-by-second, characterization of the blistering half minute shoot-out would find plausibility. For Mrs. Earp, after so many years of speculation and of controversy, finally pulled the nail out from the closet of secrets. She admitted that it was Doc Holliday and Morgan Earp who started the bloody episode on October 26, 1881, in Tombstone, when these two tempestuous pistoleros opened fire on Frank McLaury and on Billy Clanton, respectively.

8.	Josie Earp revealed that her husband Wyatt's testimony before Judge Wells Spicer was 'tainted' to enhance his claim that it was he, (Wyatt), who shot Frank McLaury in the initial fire, insinuating, at the same time, that McLaury stood across from him, (Wyatt), inside the vacant lot. Earp lied. He covered up. He had to protect his party to save them all from a hanging. What else was he to do under the circumstances?

9.	As to which of the Cowboys wounded Virgil Earp? Josie says it was either Billy Clanton or Frank McLaury. This author stands by his contention that it was Frank McLaury who shot the Marshal in the right leg calf from under his, (Frank's), horse's neck from Fremont Street.

10.	Mrs. Wyatt Earp also remarked that Tom McLaury did, in fact, have a six-shooter on him, and that, firing over the saddle of Billy Clanton's horse, McLaury caught Morgan Earp distracted momentarily by the sound of a disturbance emanating from the rear of Fly's Rooming House. In this position, Morg would have his back to the northside of Fremont Street, namely his right shoulder facing the direction of Third Street, to the west. (Tom McLaury was to eventually fall in this vicinity from the shotgun blast administered by Doc Holliday.) Hence, Morg took Tom's bullet in the right shoulder, across the back, exiting the left. Since Josie had no more to fear from legal reprisals against her deceased husband and his brothers at the time she confessed the truth about Doc and Morg's murderous gunplay near the O.K. Corral, and, having confirmed finally that Wyatt and Virgil 'clouded' their testimony before Judge Spicer in order to safeguard their party, why would Josie then attempt to promulgate a falsehood by claiming that it was really Tom who inflicted the painful right-to-left shoulder wound on Morgan? Unless, as this author believes, and as you, Ben, also advocate, that Mrs. Wyatt Earp was correct. It WAS Tom McLaury who shot Morgan Earp. It had to be.

Witness R. F. Coleman described Tom McLaury as, in part, answering the assault WITH HIS PISTOL, before he eventually collapsed.

Tombstoners, Messrs. A. C. Bilicke and J. B. W. Gardiner, testified that Tom entered Everhardy's Butcher Shop on Allen Street just before the street fight, and after a few minutes, emerged therefrom with his right pants' pocket bulging as if a revolver protruded therein.

The Earps and their legal counsel maintained throughout the Wells Spicer trial that McLaury was armed, and fired the shot that hit Morgan.

Sheriff Behan said that he did not believe McLaury to be armed. But he failed to actually search Tom. The Sheriff then allowed that McLaury could have had a six-shooter tucked in the waist band of his trousers, and he, (Behan), have "not known it".

In the final analysis, it is to Mrs. Wyatt Earp and her startling disclosures about her husband's concealment of his party's homicidal assault against the Cowboys, via the quick triggers of Doc Holliday and Morgan Earp, that this author shall defer. Josie had nothing to lose. It was time to tell the truth. She stated that Tom McLaury was Morgan Earp's attacker.

I believe it. The pieces to the puzzle have now come together.

And we have the most responsible and outstanding authority in Earpiana in the world today to thank for it....Mr. Glenn G. Boyer.

Note: Closing paragraph(s) and felicitations deleted.

Michael M. Hickey

June 10, 1991

MR. BEN T. TRAYWICK

Re: <u>Street Fight in Tombstone, Near the O.K. Corral</u>

Dear Ben:

Thank you for discussing the aforereferenced pending manuscript at length with the undersigned, particularly in the context of the final walk-up and approach to the shoot-out site on Fremont Street by the Earps and Doc Holliday, and whether the historic gunfight that followed was deliberately planned, or, whether it was, to put it in your words, an 'accident'.

Permit me to comment, as follows:

1.   Tombstone enthusiasts and novices in Earpiana, (like the undersigned author), do admit to sometimes being caught up in the 'Old Wild West' syndrome popularized by Hollywood movies, television programming, and fiction paper-back books that depict blazing six-guns in the middle of the street, with both Lawmen and Cowboys on the receiving end of death-dealing fusillades. But the truth appears to be the opposite, relevant to the survivability of the Law Officers of Tombstone during the period of the Earps. The fact is, that one just did not go around cold-bloodedly killing Peace Officers in those days, without fear of some type of serious consequence such as a trial and legal hanging, or by a lynching via some vigilante group, or a rampaging mob of mine workers claiming to belong to one of the several law-and-order citizens committees that permeated that desert sin city at the time.

2.   What all of the experts of the O.K. Corral tragedy seem to overlook is that in the days of the Earp era in Tombstone, (December, 1879 to the late spring of 1882), only Marshal Fred White appears to have been a fatality on the side of the law. (In October, 1880, he was killed by 'Curly Bill' Brocius, near the future location of the Bird Cage Theater.) Even this homicide has its bellicose advocates to the effect that 'Curly Bill's' pistol fired accidentally when the Marshal tried to take it away from the Cowboy leader. As with just about everything else in the study of Earpiana, the debate continues. For example, we do have the suspicion by Fred Dodge, the undercover agent for Wells Fargo in Tombstone, at the time, that the Marshal White shooting was not an accident, but a premeditated murder.

3.   In furtherance to the above, you pointed out to this author that another Peace Officer, Deputy Kiv Phillips, was shot down and killed in the Tombstone vicinity, by a liquored up gunman named 'Orante' on July 8, 1882. This tragic event occurred several months after the Earps were believed to have left Arizona.

4.   The 'message' to all of the foregoing commentary is that it does seem to support, to a degree, your assertion that the much-storied street fight on October 26, 1881, in the vacant lot near the O.K. Corral was probably....an accident.   Granted, the immediate days preceding the Fremont Street fracas were bristling with loud boasts, threats, and all sorts of 'macho' posturing by the Cowboys against the Earps.   But such talk was, just that, talk.   It had its immediate purpose at that specific time to enable Ike Clanton to vindicate himself in the eyes of his Cowboy confederates, who might begin to suspect that he, (Ike), had 'sold out' the Benson Stage robbers to the Earps earlier that year, in exchange for reward money.   Ike was under pressure.   He felt compelled to do something.   Rumors of his traitorous deal with Wyatt Earp were bound to infest the Tombstone Streets, and to eventually filter back to the Cowboy leadership outside of the city.   It was just a matter of time.

5.   Hence, on the day of the O.K. Corral showdown was Ike Clanton not seen to be looking for Doc Holliday in Fly's Rooming House, (where Holliday was a boarder at the time), he, Ike, armed with a rifle and a pistol?   The braggadocious Cowboy and his cattle rustling allies would be more inclined to take the risk to shoot it out with the notorious Doc Holliday, and claim self defense, than they, (Cowboys), would be to take on the likes of the City Marshal, Virgil Earp, and his noteworthy law-upholding brother, Wyatt.   To kill the latter two city officials could provoke a citizen's reprisal, whatever the claims of the Cowboys to try to justify their acts.   Again, this author makes the point that one just did not go around killing Officers of the Law in Tombstone, in those days.

6.   Therefore, when the Earp brothers and Doc Holliday were observed by Sheriff John H. Behan and the Cowboys, to be approaching the site of the gunfight on Fremont Street, no one in the Clanton-McLaury assemblage opened fire on sight.   Why?   A major reason is attributed to the previous rationale by the undersigned, about the ill-advisability of gunning down Officers of the Law in Tombstone.   Moreover, Sheriff Behan had set himself up as a reasoned arbiter, of sorts, to attempt to bring the full weight and prestige of his county office to bear on the proceedings.   The Sheriff was present.   He was assumed to have had the Cowboys in his charge.   For the Clanton-McLaury party to start shooting, would undermine the Sheriff's ability to defend the future interests of his Cowboy 'friends'.   Instead, the politics of the moment would favor Behan, should he be able to take credit directly for the prevention of bloodshed, as opposed to allowing the Earps to disarm the Clantons and the McLaurys.   Were Behan to have succeeded in bringing about a peaceful halt to the mushrooming tensions, then it would be difficult for his detractors to argue that in matters of law enforcement in Cochise County, including in the City of Tombstone, Behan commanded more respect than the Earps.   But, both Virgil and Wyatt knew this too.   They were not about to let their sleazy nemesis emerge from all of this as a hero.

7.   Lest we forget, both Ike Clanton and Tom McLaury probably had just about all of the fight 'buffaloed' out of them when Virgil and Wyatt pistol-whipped the two Cowboys in separate humiliating and painful encounters, just an hour, or two, before the Fremont Street climax.   Too, Billy Claibourne appeared to be unarmed, and was not committed to place his life on the line for his comrades.   That left only two of the five Cowboys, namely, Frank McLaury and Billy Clanton, at least equipped and physically fit to blast it out, if

necessary, with the obviously 'heeled' and formidable Earp-Holliday quartet. Such odds did not favor the Cowboys, to say the least, and would counsel against any foolhardy acts of bravado to open fire in the city streets against armed officials of law enforcement.

Besides, tomorrow would be another day.

8.   So, I ask you, Ben, was it a natural turn of events to allow the Earp-Holliday delegation to come up, so close, to the Cowboys to the extent that Wyatt would stick his pistol in Ike Clanton's belly; that Morgan Earp was reported only six feet from Billy Clanton; and that Doc Holliday was seen by an eyewitness, from across the street, to have walked up to Frank McLaury and to have 'put' his weapon to McLaury's 'stomach', then, backing up a few feet, at which time, 'the firing became general'?

The answer is YES, if you were the Cowboys and felt that the by-the-book Marshal Earp was in control of his party, holding a cane, (not a revolver), and intending only to effect a peaceful disarmament.

The answer is YES, if you found yourself staring at the loaded pistols out, and at the ready, drawn and held by the Earps and Doc Holliday, as the Marshal's party came forward. (To pull one's own gun now, in response to being 'covered' by the six-shooters of the Lawmen, so close and in front of you, would doubtless provoke and justify the said Lawmen to commence firing.)

And, the answer is YES, if you were Ike Clanton and Tom McLaury, who knew from first hand experience that the two Earp leaders, Virgil and Wyatt, were more prone to club offenders over the head to disarm them, rather than to immediately shoot to kill. After all, these were men of the law, guardians of the peace, and not a bunch of shoot-first crazies out for blood....but....

9.   Acquiescing to the armed walk-up of the reputable Virgil and Wyatt Earp is one thing. To allow the fire-breathing Doc Holliday and his quick-tempered protege, Morgan Earp, the same advantage is like signing a death warrant. Here is where everyone....everyone....including Marshal Virgil Earp, apparently miscalculated. The Cowboys, knowing of Doc's reputation as a quick-triggered duelist, were still probably assuaged by the fact that Holliday was, this time, a part of a responsible law enforcement party, bound by any and all of such covenants not to start six-gun trouble. Ditto, Morgan Earp. So, when Frank McLaury and Billy Clanton saw Doc and Morg approaching in their direction with revolvers leveled at their gut and chest, respectively, it could have still been beyond their expectations that the two Earp hotheads would initiate the conflict.

Law Officers, even special deputies, were not supposed to do such things. Period.

10.   Ben, now to the question dealing with the manner of the actual deployment of the Earp-Holliday coterie, as they passed in front of the entrance to Bauer's Union Market, where eyewitness Martha King would later testify to Morgan Earp's remark to Doc Holliday

to, "Let them have it", to which Holliday was to reply to the affirmative. Were the Earps four, walking side-by-side? Or, were two of them in front, and two behind?

Your answer to the undersigned, when addressing this matter at length during our talk, has caused me to presume that Wyatt and Virgil were in front, two abreast, followed at such a distance by Doc and Morg, that the latter two's plottings could not have easily been overheard by the older Earp brothers ahead. In a few seconds, and after the brief conversational interlude with Sheriff Behan, both Wyatt and Virgil were to turn left, (south), into the vacant lot to accost the Cowboys therein.

But, Doc Holliday and Morgan Earp were positioned to keep on going, straight ahead, where this author contends Morg ended up near the street edge of the boardwalks, and Doc, outside and to Morgan's right, on the main road itself, these two shooters threatening Billy Clanton and Frank McLaury, respectively.

11.   Yet, even when the Earp party continued to edge toward them, the Cowboys must have still hoped that Sheriff Behan's persistent exhortations to try to stop the group of Officers from moving closer would succeed. However, in front of the entrance to Fly's Boarding House, the Earps, (claims this author), pulled out their pistols. Sheriff Behan then took the proverbial 'stage left' and sought cover. The Earp party now 'had the drop' on the Cowboys. It was too late.

12.   For Virgil and for Wyatt, it was a natural act, a resource of their authority, so to speak, to gain the upper hand immediately, and to attempt to intimidate the Cowboys to avoid a shooting. It was their right, their place, as Officers in such a circumstance, to want to pull firearms first, in order to make their point, dramatically, and effectively. In this regard, the undersigned is referring more to the strategic attitude of the two Earp leaders, in that Virgil did not actually draw his revolver until the fight was well underway. The Marshal, instead, held a cane in his right hand, wielding the same aloft during the opening seconds, to theatricalize his demand that the Cowboys give up their weapons peaceably. But it is now clear, (to this author), that Doc Holliday and Morgan Earp did not consider themselves to be bound by the same disciplinary code, on that cold overcast October afternoon, 110 years ago. These two impetuous gun-toters had other things on their minds, especially Mr. Holliday. It was he who was to blow the whole case for the Earps, (including their future in the Tombstone community), by first unleashing a murderous pistol shot into the abdomen of Frank McLaury. Morgan simultaneously opened up on Billy Clanton. Young Billy's lightning reflexes sensed the attack that was coming. He knew it was kill, or be killed. He was already in the act of clearing his six-shooter to fire at Marshal Virgil Earp, standing about ten feet in front of him, when Morgan's .45 caliber bullet ripped into his left chest, throwing him backwards, thereby causing the Cowboy to shoot wildly, and to miss his target. So states Mrs. Josie Earp in Glenn G. Boyer's landmark work, I Married Wyatt Earp, that Morgan probably saved his older brother's life. Now, Morg 'cut loose' again at Billy Clanton, this second shot hitting the young Cowboy near the wrist of his, (Billy's), shooting hand, and shattering it. Ike Clanton, with all of the horror and trepidation imaginable at seeing it come to this, with his kid brother, 19-year old

Billy being overwhelmed by the deadly gunfire of the Earps, lunged at Wyatt Earp, causing Wyatt's pistol to discharge in the direction of the retreating Billy Claibourne, which bullet, in all probability, grazed the pants leg of the so-called 'Arizona Billy The Kid'.

And, as they say....the rest is history.

Sincerely,

Michael M. Hickey

"IN THE NAME OF GOD, WHERE DO WE GET SUCH MEN?"

An Editorial Tribute

To the Gunslingers of Street Fight in Tombstone, Near the O.K.Corral

It all happened in thirty seconds, with about thirty shots fired, between nine hard-cased and desperate men, with two panic-stricken horses thrown in for good measure, all of it starting in a death trap-like enclosure, a vacant lot, no more than fifteen feet wide. They stood toe-to-toe, face-to-face, with no place to run, and no place to hide. It has been the damnedest thing for this author to try to describe all of the frenetic action in that half-minute, 110 years ago, so that the reader can follow along, yet maintain a clear under-standing of who shot who?....how?....why?....while also being reminded that the whole horrific episode took only thirty seconds.

'Thirty seconds, with about thirty shots fired.' That means one shot per second, in a man-ner of speaking. In just that almost imperceptible 'blink' of time, consider that....

TOM McLAURY managed to maneuver with Billy Clanton's horse right out of the vacant lot; produce a pistol; shoot over the saddle of the horse to inflict the shoulder wound on Morgan Earp; himself, (Tom), finally taking a load of twelve buckshot charges at close range from the sawed-off shotgun wielded by Doc Holliday; yet, Tom was still able to stagger away from the bedlam to the corner of Fremont and Third Streets, where he col-lapsed.

DOC HOLLIDAY, that tempestuous duelist of the 'shoot first school', armed with shot-gun in one hand, and his trademark nickel-plated Colt pistol in the other, even shocked his own party by opening fire at point-blank range at Frank McLaury; then tried to gun down Ike Clanton as the Cowboy chief was making his escape through the front door of Fly's Boarding House; then switched weapons in the street by holstering his short barrel six-shooter, and with feet firmly planted, proceeded to pour shrapnel at the hapless Tom McLaury; and with the shotgun emptied, threw it to the ground, yanked his revolver, again, to join in the fight-ending fusillade with Morgan and Wyatt Earp against Frank McLaury, taking a shot in the back from McLaury in the process.

MORGAN EARP, the hothead, devil-may-care youngest of 'The Fighting Earps', after blast-ing Billy Clanton in the opening seconds, was hit in the right shoulder by Tom McLaury, the bullet tearing clear across Morg's back, exiting the left; Morg fell down in the street; rose right up and rejoined the gun-play; and, shoulder wound and all, fired the killing shot into Frank McLaury's brain that seemed to have terminated the hostilities.

FRANK McLAURY, no slouch himself in that most fabled Frontier showdown, was gut-shot by Doc Holliday in the very first second; was able to hang on to the reins of his spooked horse, using the animal as a protective wall, while being half-dragged to the other side of the road; pulled his pistol; fired three shots, two from under the neck of the horse; one hit Virgil Earp; one barely missed; the third creased the back of Doc Holliday; two hits out of three; not bad for a dying man, faced off, one against three, at the end of the street battle.

VIRGIL EARP, the Marshal changed his cane from his right to his left hand, pulled his gun, and, "went to fighting", but was almost immediately struck in the right leg calf by Frank McLaury's .45 caliber bullet fired from Fremont Street when Frank used his horse as a barricade; Virgil stumbled, but kept his feet, cane now in left hand, pistol in right; he returned one shot at McLaury, just missing, but probably gashing the Cowboy's horse, causing it to break away to gallop down the street; then Virgil turned on Billy Clanton and loosed three consecutive shots at the young ruffian; one hit the Cowboy in the right side beneath the twelfth rib; the second came within inches of striking its target but crashed into the side of the Harwood House when Billy abruptly lost his feet and slid to the ground; the last bullet perforated Clanton's pants leg, in the area of the right knee.

BILLY CLANTON, what mettle, what stuff, this 19-year old kid had to be made of, to be shot four times, two of which were irrefutably fatal wounds; to still unload his six-gun at the Earps, firing deliriously, wildly, but shooting back in the face of certain death and overwhelming odds; and finally, even when his emptied pistol was being wrestled from his hand by onlooker, C. S. Fly, as Billy lay gasping for breath in the bloodied dust of the Harwood House corner, this magnificent courageous youth of our Frontier past still pleaded, "give me some more cartridges".

WYATT EARP, arguably the most enduring legend in the history of the Old West, certainly its most controversial; its most storied character; love him, hate him, hero or villain; in the midst of all of that Armageddon in Tombstone, Arizona, on the afternoon of October 26, 1881, was described by eyewitness R. F. Coleman thusly, "Wyatt Earp stood up and fired in rapid succession, as cool as a cucumber, and was not hit".

In the name of God, where do we get such men?

Michael M. Hickey
Waco, Texas
August 4, 1991

BRUCE R. GREENE
Master Artist and Illustrator

"A most interesting and challenging assignment", is how Master Artist and Illustrator, Bruce R. Greene, described his three-month commission for Michael M. Hickey's controversial new book, Street Fight in Tombstone, Near the O.K. Corral.

Like any other fan of the Old West, Mr. Greene had seen his share of movies and television programs, and had read books and magazines about the famous showdown, to give him a kind of 'feel' for the thirty-second gunfight, and of how it might have happened. At least he thought he knew something about it. That is, until he took on the job for Talei Publishers, Inc.

"I sure learned a few things. I had a considerable amount of research and material to work with. There was a wealth of photographs, maps, and drawings about the old days in Tombstone that enabled me to develop a sense of theme for the characters. Once I had a profile sketch of each shooter, I was able to do the action scenes. I had already decided that the only way to do justice to the subject matter, and to the author's strong command of detail about the shoot-out, was to do all of the original artworks in oil paintings; black and white only; in 16" x 20", and in 20" x 30" sizes. All of the pictures in the book are reproduced from these actual oils. I am excited with the results", states Mr. Greene.

Born in Dallas, Texas, Bruce R. Greene, 38, attended North Mesquite High School. After graduation, he enrolled at the University of Texas, where he earned his B.F.A., (Bachelor of Fine Arts), majoring in painting and sculpting. But, amazingly, Bruce had already begun oil painting at age six. So taken with his work were his family and local art critics, that he began studies at the Dallas Museum of Fine Art. He was only eight years old. Throughout high school he took 'every available course in art' that he could lay his hands on. He often burned the midnight oil toning his artistic skills. In his private work he found solace, a sort of respite, a peace and serenity, even while the adrenaline and strong currents of creativity flowed within him.

In 1974, Bruce R. Greene married the former Janie Adams of Mesquite, Texas. Today they have three children, sons Brad, 15; Adam, 7; and a daughter Laci, 10. The family moved to Clifton, Texas, two years ago.

Well-known works by Mr. Greene are, in addition to his illustrations in Street Fight in Tombstone, Near the O.K. Corral, the highly emotive and striking 18-inch bronze sculpture he completed earlier this year of 'Susanna Dickinson', the heroine and last survivor of the legendary Battle of the Alamo. Equally moving is his depiction of a brave frontier woman, just widowed, with a thirteen-year old son, who must now face the rigors and the hardship of survival without her man in those perilous times. Mr. Greene sculpted a 'bronze' of this woman, holding a branding iron, while her boy held a calf to the ground. He named it, 'A Widow's Iron'. Mr. Greene's oil painting of the women and children of the Ute Tribe of the Southern Colorado Indian Nation, gathering wood for their home fires, in the heavy snows of winter, is typical of his passion and sensitivity for portraying the human spirit.

'The drama of life itself', will always be Bruce R. Greene's favorite subject.

AUTHOR'S SELECTED BIBLIOGRAPHY

I MARRIED WYATT EARP: by Glenn G. Boyer, 1976
The Recollections of Josephine Sarah Marcus Earp

TOMBSTONE, AN ILIAD OF THE SOUTHWEST   by Walter Noble Burns, 1927

THE FRONTIER WORLD OF DOC HOLLIDAY: by Pat Jahns, 1979
Faro Dealer from Dallas to Deadwood

UNDER COVER FOR WELLS FARGO: by Carolyn Lake, 1969
The Unvarnished Recollections of Fred Dodge

AND DIE IN THE WEST: by Paula Mitchell Marks, 1989
The Story of the O.K. Corral Gunfight.

THE EARPS OF TOMBSTONE   by Douglas D. Martin, 1959 Ed.

THE CHRONICLES OF TOMBSTONE   by Ben T. Traywick, 1986

THE EARPS TALK   by Alford E. Turner, 1982 Ed.

THE EARP BROTHERS OF TOMBSTONE: by Frank Waters, 1976 Ed.
The Story of Mrs. Virgil Earp

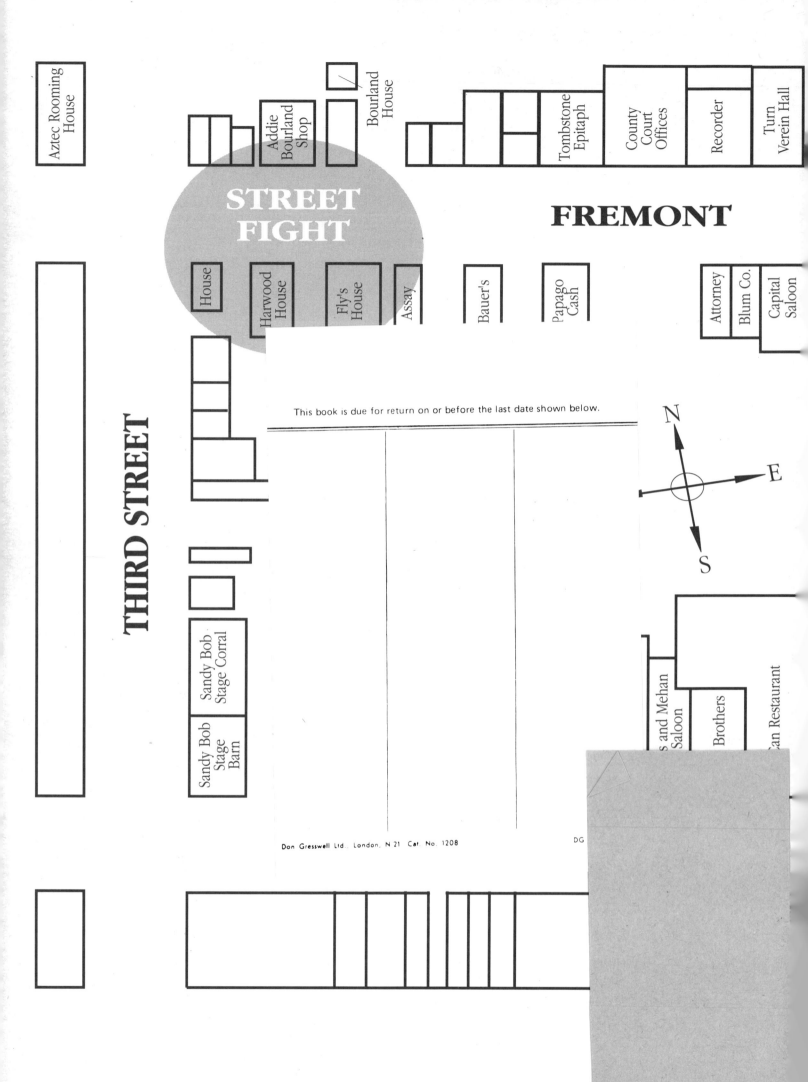

AZTEC ROOMING HOUSE

STREET FIGHT

FREMONT

Addie Bourland Shop

Bourland House

Tombstone Epitaph

County Court Offices

Recorder

Turn Verein Hall

House

Harwood House

Fly's House

Assay

Bauer's

Papago Cash

Attorney

Blum Co.

Capital Saloon

THIRD STREET

Sandy Bob Stage Corral

Sandy Bob Stage Barn

s and Mehan Saloon

Brothers

an Restaurant

N

E

S

This book is due for return on or before the last date shown below.